"In this book, Stephen Wayne, one of the most astute scholars of the presidency, presents a historically informed analysis of President Biden's first year and a half in office. Wayne's sophisticated yet readily accessible analysis guides the reader through Biden's transition into office, the successes and failures of his legislative agenda, and his foreign policy challenges. If you want to understand how the Biden presidency works, how it has dealt with its successes and setbacks, and its place in the modern presidency, this is a book you should read."

James P. Pfiffner, *George Mason University*

THE BIDEN PRESIDENCY

This book is among the first serious looks at the first 18 months of the Biden administration and its many challenges. From a tortured transition to a raging pandemic, a fragile economy, and the threat of international insecurity, Joe Biden entered office at a time even more fraught than that he faced as a new vice president. Confronting a nation divided sharply along political, cultural, and sociodemographic lines, Biden and Kamala Harris promised to unify the country, change the tone in Washington, mend fences with allies, and "build back better" a world assailed from stem to stern. This book assesses the successes and shortfalls of the Biden administration's first 18 months in office, putting all in perspective of the current state of democracy in America. Intended to introduce students of American government to the person (Biden) and the institution (presidency) within a particular system (separation of powers), this book will appeal broadly to citizens, media, and general interest readers in the United States and abroad.

Stephen J. Wayne is Professor of Government Emeritus at Georgetown University. A Washington-based "insider" for more than 50 years, Wayne is frequently quoted by White House journalists and regularly appears on television and radio news shows. He has written or edited 12 books, published in 31 editions and more than 100 articles, chapters, and reviews that have appeared in professional journals, scholarly compilations, newspapers, and magazines.

THE BIDEN PRESIDENCY

POLITICS, POLICY, AND POLARIZATION

STEPHEN J. WAYNE

Routledge
Taylor & Francis Group

NEW YORK AND LONDON

Cover image: lev radin/shutterstock

First published 2023
by Routledge
605 Third Avenue, New York, NY 10158

and by Routledge

4 Park Square, Milton Park, Abingdon, Oxon, OX14 4RN

Routledge is an imprint of the Taylor & Francis Group, an informa business

© 2023 Stephen J. Wayne

The right of Stephen J. Wayne to be identified as author of this work has been asserted in accordance with sections 77 and 78 of the Copyright, Designs and Patents Act 1988.

Library of Congress Cataloging-in-Publication Data
Names: Wayne, Stephen J., author.
Title: The Biden presidency: politics, policy, and polarization/Stephen J. Wayne.
Description: New York, NY: Routledge, 2023. | Includes bibliographical references
   and index.
Identifiers: LCCN 2022015297 (print) | LCCN 2022015298 (ebook) |
   ISBN 9781032010076 (paperback) | ISBN 9781032010687 (hardback) |
   ISBN 9781003176978 (ebook)
Subjects: LCSH: Biden, Joseph R., Jr. | United States—Politics and
   government—2021– | Political culture—United States—History—21st century. |
   Presidents—United States—History—21st century. | Presidents—United States—
   Election—2020.
Classification: LCC E916 .W39 2023 (print) | LCC E916 (ebook) | DDC 973.934—
   dc23/eng/20220330
LC record available at https://lccn.loc.gov/2022015297
LC ebook record available at https://lccn.loc.gov/2022015298

ISBN: 978-1-032-01068-7 (hbk)
ISBN: 978-1-032-01007-6 (pbk)
ISBN: 978-1-003-17697-8 (ebk)

DOI: 10.4324/9781003176978

Typeset in Galliard
by Apex CoVantage, LLC

Dedicated to Cheryl

Contents

Photos, Tables, Boxes, and Comparative Capsules

Photos

Tables

Boxes

Comparative Capsules

Preface

Setting the Stage for Biden's Presidency: Conditions, Contestations, and Reactions

- A pandemic that prompted early in-person and absentee voting more than in past presidential elections, 14 million more Democrats registered than Republicans;
- an election in which some state administrators of the voting process and the tabulators of the results were challenged, cajoled, threatened, and eventually lost their authority to oversee voting and determine the official outcome;
- a disputed election outcome in several states that was contested for years after the actual voting ended;
- a riot at the Capitol as Congress was certifying the states' electoral votes followed by a second presidential impeachment of Donald J. Trump;
- public relief that Joseph R. Biden, Jr., had won the 2020 presidential election;
- an inauguration in which the public was asked to observe events virtually, not in person;
- a deeply and widely polarized electorate and two major party candidates whose personalities, politics, and policy views were antithetical to one another;
- public approval of Biden's conduct and behavior during his first 100 days in office;
- favorable evaluation of the president's initial executive actions and policy proposals;
- positive job approval ratings in the first six months of Biden's presidency;

- a decline in public support amid rising prices, supply chain problems, and the continuing pandemic from July 2021 through July 19, 2022;
- strong Republican opposition to mandates on vaccinations, testing, and mask-wearing advice;
- increased public fears of inflation and frustration over lack of desired products, services, travel, and live entertainment.

Political Perceptions and Personal Characteristics of Candidate and Then President Joe Biden

- A candidate who initially was not expected to survive, much less win the Democratic nomination at the beginning of the campaign;
- the oldest person ever elected president of the United States, who received more votes from young voters than older ones;
- an experienced politician in an anti-politician age with a woman of color as his running mate;
- a presidential candidate who aroused less passion, less emotion, and less fervent support than his opponent but also did not evoke the negative criticism of the previous 2016 Democratic nominee, Hillary Clinton;
- a person whose manner, actions, rhetoric, and promises contrasted sharply with those of his predecessor and who strove to emphasize the differences.

Goals, Outline, and Contents of the Biden Presidency: Politics, Policy, and Polarization

This book is primarily a description and analysis of the first 18 months of the Biden presidency. It summarizes the consequences of the 2020 election for Biden, examines the transition, and evaluates his administration's performance in office. It also discusses the external environment that he had to address but could not control. Continuing and anticipated issues with which President Biden may have to deal are noted as well.

The organization of the text appears in the table of contents. There are six boxes that detail events, problems, policy proposals, and legislation enacted by one or both chambers of the 117th Congress; 11 small capsules that compare and contrast Biden and Trump's partisan policy positions and activities, and their successes and failures; 17 tables and one appendix that contain quantitative and descriptive data, as well as organizational charts of parts of the Executive Office of the President and 14 photographs.

Part I summarizes Biden's pre-presidential activities. Chapter 1 focuses on the 2020 presidential election, describing Biden's campaign promises, electoral support, and the strategies he used to win. Chapter 2 details his transition to power: how he overcame his predecessor's resistance to the requirements of the 1963 *Presidential Transition Act*, which prevented Biden's representatives from meeting with government officials for three weeks and, in some cases, even longer. The chapter also describes how Biden and his advisors organized the transition; coped with internal Democratic pressures to nominate particular candidates for office; achieved diversity by appointing more women, people of color, and ethnic minorities; and set the priorities for his domestic policy agenda. During the transition, Biden's senior aides also planned and orchestrated his first ten days in office. Little was left to chance.

Part II examines Biden's first 100 days in office: his domestic policy objectives, the strategy he adopted for interacting with Congress, and his successes and failures in achieving part of his policy agenda. Chapter 3 looks at how his first ten days were planned and orchestrated: what the president tried to do, his legislative initiatives and executive actions, and the evaluation of his performance during this period by the American people.

Chapter 4 turns to partisan politics and presidential–congressional relations. It examines areas of conflict and cooperation between and within the parties, the compromises that were made to gain sufficient support to enact Biden's policy objectives, the president's early legislative achievements and failures, and the agenda that lay ahead. Chapter 5 looks at his approach to foreign affairs, his administration's geographic emphases, ongoing diplomatic relations, and the framework Biden used to shape a foreign policy that was different from his predecessor's. The people chosen to guide his policy, the organizations they led, and their relations with their counterparts from other countries, friends and foes alike, are also described.

Part III details Biden's relations with the major institutions of American national government: Congress, the executive branch, and the legal system. The first chapter on Congress, Chapter 6, addresses problems that the president and his congressional party faced in a diverse, somewhat discordant, ideologically polarized, and closely divided Congress. It also discusses Biden's institutional and personal difficulties in dealing with two distinctive legislative bodies as well as with the enlarged egos and primary motivations of members of Congress when they considered and voted on legislation, their reelection, personal beliefs, and the need to satisfy people who voted for them, not nonvoters or political opponents. The chapter also examines the limits and opportunities for exercising presidential power, the strategies that can be used to extend that power, and the way in which the president pursued his first major legislative priority, *The American Rescue Plan Act of 2021*. Biden's personal style, modes of interaction, the major legislative issues that divided policy makers, and the White House's role in dealing with Congress and mobilizing public pressure on it are discussed as well. Chapter 7 describes the legislative outcomes, what and how the compromises were made, the president's role in negotiating them, and the proposals included in final bills that were enacted, partially successful, delayed, or failed. It also notes other significant legislation enacted into law.

In Chapter 8, the organization, operation, and principal aides selected for senior White House and top Executive Office positions are detailed as are the imagery designed to contrast Biden's presidency from Trump's, the problems that arose in his predecessor's administration that Biden wanted to avoid, the professional and personal behavior that Biden adopted on a day-to-day basis, and the ethical rules he imposed on his staff are detailed. In addition, the vice president's role and activities are explored along with the political ramifications that accompanied Kamala Harris's visibility and performance in office and her future electability as a candidate for the presidency. The chapter concludes with a description of the First Lady and Second Gentleman's functions.

Chapter 9 discusses the chief executive's role in theory and practice. A proponent of government, a merit-based civil service system, and strong management skills, Biden initially had to overcome his predecessor's animosity toward the "deep state" and the shape and the size of the civil service he left. Encouraging loyal, experienced, and knowledgeable public servants to federal employment, identifying and removing Trump's political appointees, and the consequences of confirmation delays, which exacerbated Biden's start-up activities, are assessed as are recent presidents' dependence on the Office of Management and Budget (OMB) to oversee, coordinate, and regulate executive department and agency decision-making in its role as the president's surrogate and advocate. Also noted are some of the management problems that Biden faced and his use of executive authority to deal with them and other policy implementation issues.

The final chapter in this part of the book, Chapter 10, looks at the judicial system, a system that has become increasingly important because of the number of legal challenges to elections, legislation, and the criminal allegations and charges against Trump's campaign associates, administration officials, and the former president himself. Biden had accused Trump's Department of Justice as being improperly and unethically partisan. He wanted to establish a more independent relationship between the White House and the department, but tensions still were evident. Attorney General Merrick Garland objected to some personnel suggested by the White House to head principal divisions within the department and legal positions it advocated on contentious political issues which landed in the courts. Despite these initial disagreements, the department became a critical vehicle on which the administration relied to protect minority voting rights after the failure of national voting rights legislation.

Part IV discusses the public dimension of the Biden presidency: the communication model the administration adopted and the public relations campaigns it waged. Chapter 11 focuses on the structure and operation of the White House's outreach activities, describing the president's style and rhetoric, where, when, and in what form communications were conducted, venues used, and the messages targeted to specific groups. It also examines how the administration used polling data, how it interacted with the news media, and the press coverage it received.

Chapter 12 turns to public opinion and presidential popularity. It notes how the administration benefited in its first six months and then how adverse economic, social, and political conditions negatively affected perceptions of the Biden presidency. The chapter concludes with Gallup Poll data on public opinion of the president.

Part V looks at the administration's evolving doctrine in foreign policy, and its accomplishments and failures. Thus far, the most controversial foreign policy decision that Biden has made, the ending of America's military involvement in Afghanistan, is discussed in Chapter 13 as well as other foreign policy issues.

Biden's achievements and failures are evaluated in the final chapter. How well has the president met his campaign promises, achieved his original goals, and dealt with unanticipated conditions and events? How well and with what effect has President Biden distinguished himself and his administration from his predecessor, Donald Trump? To what extent has Biden helped or hurt his ability to govern for the rest of his time in office? Stay tuned.

ACKNOWLEDGMENTS

I would like to thank my wife, Cheryl Beil, who encouraged me to write this book; my brother-in-law, Marshall Beil, who helped me improve the substance and writing of the manuscript; Barbara Block, who let me stay in her apartment while recovering from pneumonia to self-isolate myself from COVID-19; and all the people at Taylor & Francis: Jennifer Knerr, senior editor, whose encouragement, support, and detailed comments helped me to improve the manuscript greatly, Jacqueline Dorsey, editorial assistant, who helped acquire the photos for the book, and Apex CoVantage, LLC, company that facilitated the transmittal of the manuscript into a book.

PART I

THE PRELIMINARIES

CHAPTER 1

THE 2020 ELECTIONS AND THEIR CONSEQUENCES

The elections of 2020 set the stage for the presidency of Joseph R. Biden, Jr. The race for president lasted almost four years. Donald J. Trump started his reelection campaign almost immediately after his 2016 election victory, even though he faced minimal opposition within his own party. Republican members of Congress touted his claims and acknowledged his leadership, but most went their own way in performing their legislative responsibilities and deciding how to vote.

Twenty-nine Democrats seeking their party's nomination began announcing their candidacies as early as 2017 and 2018 with the bulk of them tossing their hats in the ring in the spring of 2019. They raised and spent huge amounts of money, $4.1 billion. Michael Bloomberg had the largest self-funded war chest, $1.1 billion, most of which he spent between November 2019 and March 2020. Biden raised $1 billion, most of which he received after he was the acknowledged victor of the Democratic nomination. Trump's total expenditures were $812 million, but early spending diminished the amount he had left in the critical last weeks of the presidential election.

Despite Trump's early start, most of the nomination campaign took place from mid-2019 through election day in 2020 with Trump holding rallies and spending extensively on television and online media. The race for the Democratic nomination ended in early April after Biden won resounding victories in the South Carolina and Super Tuesday (March 3, 2020) primaries. He extended his lead over the winner of the early, post-calendar caucuses and primaries, Bernie Sanders, whose lead in Democratic convention delegates frightened traditional and more moderate Democrats. They concluded that Biden was the more electable nominee and endorsed him after they dropped out of the race. Sanders conceded

DOI: 10.4324/9781003176978-2

in mid-April and said he would support Biden, thereby ending the nomination phase of the 2020 presidential election.

In early March, Trump had been leading in the pre-election polls. He had raised a lot of money for his campaign. A strong economy with low unemployment rates and little inflation, a rising stock market, and a growing economy aided his quest for reelection, but Trump's rhetoric and executive actions, his social media posts and ads, and his personal tweets reinforced his leadership style which Democrats, Independents, and some Republicans found offensive and objectionable—words and actions that did not conform to their expectations of presidential behavior.

By the middle of March 2020, Trump faced what was to become his largest obstacle, one he was unable to surmount: the rapid spread of COVID-19. Trump belittled the threat of the virus and its harmful effects. During the campaign and before the first debate, Trump was infected with the virus. He did not reveal it publicly until it became severe, and he was rushed to Walter Reed National Military Medical Center in nearby Maryland for treatment.

While being infected, he mocked Biden for wearing a mask, interacted with White House staff, attended out-of-town events, and spoke with

Photo 1.1 *Biden and Trump exchange heated words in their first presidential debate in September 2020*
Source: *AP Photo/Morry Gash, Pool*

reporters on Air Force One—all without a mask, thereby spreading the virus among his supporters, White House staff, and others.

The Trump administration's slow and inadequate response to the health threat and its negative economic impact undermined the president's election campaign. People were frightened. COVID-19 dominated the news. This enabled the Democrats to energize their base, attract Independents, and even gain the support of some Republicans who saw Trump as a danger to the country and his party.

The 2020 presidential campaign focused on the candidates' style of leadership and the policies they would pursue as president. Trump's unconventional manner, unpredictable actions, emotive and controversial rhetoric, blame-shifting accusations, and self-interested, self-promoting, self-aggrandizing behavior energized his base but also his opponents, albeit in different ways. Biden was seen as safer, less doctrinaire, more responsible, more deliberative, more predictable, and more empathetic by his supporters, but weaker, wordier, older, and more like a traditional Washington politician by his opponents. Although partisan voters continued to support their party's nominees, most of whom reflected their ideological beliefs, Independents voted for the Democratic presidential ticket more than they did in 2016. Biden was not viewed negatively, as was Hillary Clinton.

For the American public, the pandemic, the economy, and the president's inconsistent, inaccurate, and unresponsive statements and actions became the most important problem the country faced. Racial demonstrations directed toward harsh and unlawful policing fueled the partisan divide, reduced trust and confidence in government, and affected the content, tone, and amount of campaign news coverage, mostly to the president's disadvantage.

Unsuccessful leadership during crises had led to the defeat of the last three other incumbents who lost their reelection bids: Herbert Hoover, Jimmy Carter, and George H. W. Bush. Trump's leadership style also had a lot to do with his defeat. His rhetoric energized his base but turned off others; his calls for law and order during and after racial demonstrations, his defense of white supremacist groups, the constant turbulence within his administration, and his contention that if he lost it was because of fraud inflamed Democrats, concerned Independents and some Republicans, and contributed to larger turnout and voting behavior.

Two-thirds of eligible citizens in the population voted. Two-thirds of these voters cast their ballots early, either in person or by mail. Biden received 81 million popular votes, 7 million more than Trump. He also received a substantial victory in the Electoral College by the same margin Trump had won by four years earlier (309 to 232).

When the presidential election results became clear four days after election day, Trump refused to concede. He contended that the vote in states that were close was rigged and blamed the false results on biased programming of voting machines, fraudulent and miscounted mail-in votes, and tabulation errors. Lawyers supporting Trump instituted 61 lawsuits in the key battleground states in which Biden's margin of victory was smallest. All but one of Trump's legal challenges were dismissed by federal and state judges for lack of evidence.

Nonetheless, Trump contested the election outcome. He rallied his supporters in Washington on January 6, 2021, the day Congress certified each state's electoral vote. At the rally, Trump repeated his claims of a rigged election and besieged his adherents to march to the Capitol to stop the electoral vote count and reverse the outcome. He also pressured Vice President Mike Pence, the president of the Senate, to nullify the electoral vote of some states and accept new slates of electors that Republican legislatures controlling those states would send to Washington. The vice president said he did not have the authority to do so.

The attempts to overturn Biden's victory, the January 6 insurrection of the Capitol, and the president's behavior during the riot when he watched the events unfold on television for hours and claimed that they demonstrated justifiable, widespread anger over the election, led to Trump's second impeachment by the House of Representatives and trial in the Senate. The 57 to 43 vote to convict him fell ten votes short of the required two-thirds necessary to do so.

Despite Biden's victory, the 2020 elections were not a huge Democratic sweep. The Republicans gained seats in the House of Representatives but not majority control; they lost three seats in the Senate, which ended up evenly divided after two special elections in Georgia that were held in early January. The GOP increased its legislative control of two more states.

The electoral returns testified to a still divided nation and a wide and deeply polarized political environment. Voting patterns in the electorate were evident among women and men, racial and ethnic minorities and whites, young and old, college and non-college educated, cities, suburbs, and rural areas. They were also evident, but to a lesser extent, in the issues people deemed most important.

Comparative Capsule 1.1	Major Election Assets
BIDEN	**TRUMP**
Pandemic	Passion for candidate
Dislike of Trump's personality and performance as president	Patriotic and xenophobic appeal
Women, minorities, young voters	White, rural, older voters

During and after the election, Biden had promised to try to unify the country; reduce rancor and discord; elevate trust, transparency, and truthfulness in government; revive the economy; control the pandemic; and improve racial relations—a tall order, to be sure, given the electoral divide.

The 2020 elections did not produce the euphoria that often accompanies a new president's victory. There was little halo effect. Security concerns, racial issues, a pandemic that infected millions and killed hundreds of thousands, a faltering economy amid growing unemployment, and behaviors and actions that threatened democratic elections and government generated fear and loathing rather than enthusiasm, although there was relief that Biden had won.

Had Trump not contested the election results, not extended his campaign beyond election day, delayed the government transition, attended the inauguration, urged his base to support the new president, and facilitated the transition, the new president's assumption of office would have been less contentious and more celebratory and the need to move quickly less urgent. But Trump continued to be a bitter loser, foster dissent, and exercise sway over his Republican base and elected officials. His behavior left the Biden administration little choice but to stick to his and his party's policy agenda rather than to try to bring the country together.

Nonetheless, a majority of Americans approved of the election results, Biden's transfer of power, and the job he was doing as president. Initially, he had to overcome adverse circumstances to lead, to govern, and to establish his presidential status.

Depending on the date of the election, there are 75 to 79 days for a new administration to get up to speed, take over the executive branch, and respond quickly to any national emergencies, anticipated or unanticipated. In 2020, there were 77.

In 1963, Congress enacted the *Presidential Transition Act* to provide for the orderly transfer of power. That legislation requires the president to designate a transition coordinator, establish White House and agency transition teams, and report to the Senate and House committees overseeing the administration of government, and to do so several months before the election. After the results of the election are official, the head of the General Services Administration (GSA) must provide space, equipment, and funds to the newly elected president, vice president, and their staffs to begin their preparation for governing. In 2020, Congress appropriated $9.9 million for transition funding.[1]

Since the enactment of the transition law, incumbent presidents have for the most part facilitated the transfer of power.[2] President Trump did not. He refused to concede the election, had party officials challenge the vote in several states, and tried also to impede congressional certification of the Electoral College vote. Bob Woodward and Robert Costa tell the story of what he tried to do, to whom, and with what outcome in their book *Peril*.[3]

Transitional Issues

President Trump claimed that fraudulent voting, partisan machine programming, and other illegal activities skewed the count and produced false results. He refused to acknowledge defeat, fired an executive branch

DOI: 10.4324/9781003176978-3

official in the Department of Homeland Security who acknowledged the honesty and validity of the 2020 vote, and prevented the head of the GSA from starting the transition to a new administration.

Although several of his former senior advisors (chief of staff General John F. Kelly, national security advisors John Bolton and Lt. General H.R. McMaster, and a few Republican governors) criticized the president's actions to delay the transition, stating that they endangered the country's security, most elected Republican officials remained silent; they were fearful of Trump's wrath, his influence with the GOP base, and his threat to run again in 2024 and recruit loyal Trump challengers to their renomination if they opposed his claim of victory. More than one month after the election was over, only 26 out of 220 Republican lawmakers in Congress acknowledged Biden as the legitimate winner.[4]

During this contentious postelection dispute, President Trump remained in the White House, held a few public events, did not meet with his coronavirus task force as the virus surged across the country, spoke with a few conservative commentators, and played golf: lots of it. Mainstream news media condemned the president's behavior; Democrats were furious. The electorate was unnerved.

Biden initially tried to ignore Trump's misleading claims about the election and his administration's obstruction of the transition, saying "I find this more embarrassing for the country than debilitating of my ability to get started."[5] Eventually, however, the president-elect and his advisors launched a public relations campaign directed at business and public interest groups, Republican and Democratic party leaders, and the general public to inform them of the dangers of a new administration taking office without necessary information on the critical issues, intelligence briefings,[6] and knowledge of the government's COVID-19 test capacity and its plans to distribute vaccines. The president-elect could not even begin the process of obtaining security clearances for his proposed nominees, much less protect his transition staff's internal communication network from those who wanted to embarrass, derail, or profit from the political upheaval that followed the 2020 presidential election.

The Biden campaign to pressure the government to cooperate worked. Trump finally relented. In a Saturday evening tweet on November 21, 2020, almost three weeks after election day, Trump indicated that he would not prevent government officials from meeting with Biden's representatives and briefing them on pending issues. Two days later, Emily Murphy, General Services Administrator, formally acknowledged Biden as president-elect, thereby permitting the Trump–Biden transition to proceed.

Still, some of Trump's political appointees failed to comply with the letter and spirit of the transition law and Trump's reluctant approval. Top officials in the Department of Defense, Office of Management and Budget (OMB), Environmental Protection Agency, and the Voice of America delayed their meetings with the president-elect's transition teams, some until the new calendar year. Most classified briefings, which had to be held in secure government facilities, were suspended; written requests for information from Biden's transition staff went unanswered. The failure of the OMB to provide financial data on government operations and private sector contracts further hampered the Biden team's efforts. Moreover, when sessions between civil servants and transition teams did occur, some of Trump's political appointees attended, thereby politicizing the information that Biden's representatives received even further. There was no meeting between Biden and Trump and no interaction with Trump's White House staff.

There were other problems with Biden's transitioning to the presidency. After the election, the Trump administration tried to reclassify numerous agency positions from political to nonpolitical to allow the "burrowing-in" of some of Trump's operatives into the civil service. This practice was not unique to Trump; Barack Obama and his predecessors did so as well.

The staffing issue was further aggravated by the Trump administration's failure to identify the converted career positions to which political appointees had been placed, forcing the transition teams to do so on their own. They had to evaluate the qualifications of "burrowed-in" officials and make sure the Trump administration's appointment process did not violate the rules of merit-based hiring and promotions.

Biden promised to reverse the new procedures that Trump had promulgated for the civil service, remove unqualified personnel he had appointed, and fill the vacancies he and his department secretaries had purposively left. Biden also pledged to increase the number and improve the morale of government employees and depoliticize the system.[7]

Organizing the Biden Transition

Beginning transition planning in March 2020 after he became the likely Democratic nominee, Biden asked his longtime friend and former senator, Ted Kaufman, to suggest a transition director. Kaufman recommended

Jeff Zients, a former member of the Obama administration and Harvard professor. Zients initially assembled a staff of about 450, which included 200 volunteers, which grew in size to about 1,500. Biden's transition team was much larger and more diverse than Trump's.[8]

Forty groups, including organized policy areas, communications, congressional outreach, and fundraising, were created. There were also IT and security specialists on the staff. The policy groups were tasked with informing the president-elect and his top advisors of the major issues confronting government departments and agencies, including their budgetary and personnel needs, converting Biden's campaign promises into legislative policies and executive actions, and suggesting candidates for low-, middle-, and top-level positions in the administration. The new administration wanted to "hit the ground running" with as many people in place as quickly as possible. Former government officials who had served in previous Democratic administrations, domestic and foreign policy experts, and students of public service were asked to brief the teams before Trump allowed government officials to do so.

The transition operated virtually during the pandemic. More than 8,000 interviews were conducted with potential candidates for office; 130 files for major political appointments were given to the president-elect. More than half of the candidates were women, and almost half were people of color.[9]

The final decision makers on White House and cabinet-level positions were the president-elect, the vice president elect, and Biden's senior advisors. Given the large number of appointees, the selection process continued after the transition and was conducted by the White House Office of Presidential Personnel in conjunction with the soon-to-be nominated department secretaries who were given considerable discretion to choose their personal aides; the State Department officials advised on non-prestigious ambassadorships from a pool of its senior foreign service officers, while the key ambassadorships were to be determined by the president.

In deciding whom to appoint, Biden went with his gut. He valued people who had already demonstrated governing skills—collaborators, not instigators. The president-elect's preference for public service experience, however, clashed with his promise of diversity. Biden's initial choices of senior advisors and cabinet secretaries, many of whom had worked in previous Democratic administrations, raised the concerns among diversity advocates that they were not getting the representation they were promised and deserved.

Internal Democratic Politics

As candidate, Biden had pledged an administration that "looked like America." Ethnic, racial, gender, and other social groups pressured him to keep his word. They mounted letter-writing campaigns, issued their concerns, suggested candidates for executive branch appointments, and requested meetings with Biden, Harris, and senior presidential aides involved in the selection decision-making. Some even went public with their demands. The activity of these groups highlighted the unifying challenges Biden faced within his own party. The need for diversity reduced his range of choices, particularly as the process progressed.

Internal politics are endemic to presidential transitions. The groups that claimed to have had the largest electoral influence on Biden's victory exercised the most pressure: African Americans, the Hispanic community, women's groups, and some environmental organizations. Asian Americans, Jewish and Muslim groups, and the LGBTQ community lobbied less forcibly and publicly.

Here are a few examples of the competition that occurred within Biden's coalition of electoral supporters during the transition on appointments to office, competition that continued even after he took office.

Energy Producers and Workers Versus Environmental Activists

Biden had promised to reduce the use of fossil fuels during his campaign. He said, if elected, he would pursue technologies that could capture the leakage of methane from existing pipes, wells, and fracking; eliminate tax subsidies for the oil and gas industry; and stop the issuance of permits for drilling on federal lands. He also did not want the United States to invest in or encourage fossil fuel projects.

The transition to renewable energy was hampered by labor issues. There were more jobs, higher wages, and more influential labor unions in the fossil fuel industry than there were in solar and wind energy. Senator Joe Manchin, a key Democratic vote in an equally divided upper chamber, represented a coal-producing state, West Virginia, and naturally was leery of restrictions on fossil fuel production.

Jobs versus climate change were tough issues for Democrats to resolve. Environmentalists opposed the selection of executives and representatives from fossil fuel companies; labor unions supported them. Much of the fossil fuel exploration and production abroad occurred in less-developed countries that needed the revenue it provided. Leaving that market to China and Russia would increase their influence in that part of the world. Biden had to resolve these dilemmas to the satisfaction of environmentalists, American workers, and foreign policy experts.

Small Farmers Versus Big Agriculture

There were many candidates proposed for Secretary of Agriculture. Trump's trade policies with China, food shortages and disruptions during the pandemic, low prices for dairy products, and family farm bankruptcies had produced much anguish within farming communities. African American groups promoted the candidacy of Representative Marcia Fudge (OH); business groups and the National Farmers Union supported Tom Vilsack (IA), a former governor of Iowa and advisor to the Biden campaign; and liberal Democrats from the West backed former senator Heidi Heitkamp (ND).

Although Biden leaned to Vilsack, who had extensive managerial experience as Obama's agriculture secretary, opposition to his selection came from liberals who charged that he had been a proponent of agricultural consolidation and had supported policies that favored big business, such as the meatpacking industry. Vilsack had also been a million-dollar-a-year lobbyist for the U.S. Dairy Export Council.

Small farmers and environmental and consumer groups also opposed Vilsack's nomination, but for different reasons. African Americans were upset that Vilsack fired a Black employee when he was Secretary of Agriculture in the Obama administration after she was quoted out of context by a conservative blogger. (Vilsack subsequently apologized and offered her the job back, which she did not take.) The head of the Retail, Wholesale, and Department Store Union complained that the former secretary had approved a rule that increased the pace of slaughtering animals, aiding meatpacking companies at the expense of the health and safety of their workers. The National Farmers Union contended that his appointment would reduce meat and other food shortages. Republican Senator Charles Grassley (IA) voiced his support for Vilsack, while reformers argued that he would not institute the changes that small farmers so desperately needed.

Photo 2.1 *Former Senator Heidi Heitkamp (ND)*
Source: AP Photo/J. Scott Applewhite, File

Photo 2.2 *Secretary of Agriculture Tom Vilsack (IA)*
Source: AP Photo/David Zalubowski

Photo 2.3 *Congresswoman Marcia Fudge (OH)*
Source: Tom Williams/CQ Roll Call via AP Images

Moderates Versus Progressives

The "politics as usual" approach to policymaking versus the need for innovative change, particularly for those at the lower end of the social-economic scale, evident during the Democratic primaries, continued throughout the transition and into the new administration. Moderates tended to value candidates with public service experience, knowledge of policy issues, and governing skills to get the job done. They were leery of those who proposed major, rapid, and costly social policies. In contrast, progressive Democrats wanted reforms that help the needy and the neglected. They saw new faces, new ideas, and new energy as criteria that should play an important role in the selection process.

As a moderate, lifelong public servant, Biden desired team players, not policy rivals, and certainly not a government of strangers that characterized the first year of Trump's presidency. He wanted people who did not need on-the-job training, given the magnitude of the health, economic, environmental, and political crises that the country was facing. He viewed rapport as a critical attribute.

The president-elect also wanted to avoid the turnover problems, divisive politics, and management chaos that beset the Trump presidency.[10]

In Trump's first year in office, more than one-third of the top appointees in the White House and Executive Office of the President (EOP) left on their own or were fired. Almost half of the president's cabinet turned over by the end of his second year in office.[11]

Biden's preference for experienced government decision makers was resented by campaign workers, especially younger ones, who found themselves at a competitive disadvantage. Campaign operatives contended that their political loyalty, electoral selling skills, and personal interactions with voters provided a better sense of what Democratic partisans wanted, needed, and expected than did the perspectives of veterans who worked in previous Democratic campaigns and administrations, particularly those who took high-paying private sector jobs when the Democrats were out of power.

The moderate versus progressive quest for influence in the Biden administration ended in the same way as did the Democratic nomination campaign: the moderates won out. Biden chose senior White House personnel and major department secretaries with proven skills that the president-elect had observed in his more than 50 years in government. He wanted to appoint crisis managers not policy experts, compromisers not ideologues, decision makers with an instinct for making the right political judgments.

Corporate America Versus the General Public

One of the most contentious complaints voiced by the general public over the years has been the perceived influence of big business on the formulation and implementation of public policy.[12] Revolving-door politics has been a root cause of this issue. Many senior executives come into government from the private sector when a new administration takes over and leave it to return to higher-paying jobs in that sector. Their value to companies increases because of their personal contacts, substantive policy knowledge, and experience in the agencies in which they worked.

Most Americans believe that the revolving door is the vehicle that drives special interest politics. The representatives of firms with large government contracts are particularly suspect by public interest groups such as Common Cause, the Center for Responsive Politics (opensecrets.org), Public Citizen, and the Revolving Door Project on the grounds that the government's hiring of people from private industry advantages those organizations with the most resources, strongest leadership, and largest electoral constituencies to influence public policy. During the Biden transition, progressives opposed the appointment of a senior member of the Obama White House who advised cuts in social welfare spending, a big-city mayor who they claimed mishandled a police shooting in 2014, and the head of California's Air Resources Board who favored "cap and trade" emission standards that benefited industry but neglected poor and minority neighborhoods.

Another potential revolving-door issue concerned General Lloyd Austin, nominated for Secretary of Defense. After Austin left the military in 2013, he served on the boards of Raytheon Technologies, one the largest defense contractors; Nucor, the biggest U.S. steel manufacturer; and Tenet, a major health-care provider. Would these affiliations affect Austin's judgment as secretary? Moreover, Austin's appointment would require Congress to waive the legal requirement that the Secretary of Defense must not be an active-duty member of the military for seven years prior to appointment, a requirement designed to ensure civilian control of the country's armed forces. (Former Secretary of Defense James Mattis received such a waiver in 2017.) Women's groups were also unhappy that Biden did not pick Michèle Flournoy, a leading defense official in the Obama administration, to head the Defense Department.

Fierce competition within the party for top positions and for Senate confirmation of the nominees motivated some candidates to amend their résumés, downplaying their corporate connections, and even deleting some of their tweets that could influence opposition inside and outside the party. One CEO had his company's website altered to deemphasize his company's relationships with China; another candidate removed overly partisan tweets about the Trump administration that made her a target of Republicans.[13]

Ethical Considerations

Biden, sensitive to the charge that he was re-creating another "old boys network," required all transition staffers to pledge that they and their families would not benefit from the policy and personnel advice they gave to the president-elect. Registered lobbyists serving on the transition teams were prohibited from being involved on any issue on which they represented private sector clients for 12 months before and after the Biden transition. Senior aides to the president who had worked for large corporations, investment firms, and technology companies had to recuse themselves from any subject involving their former employers. All political appointees were expected to adhere to a code of conduct.

As president-elect, Biden also said that he would not appoint family members to government positions. He was sensitive to charges that his son, Hunter, profited from business connections in the Ukraine and China during the time Biden was vice president. The publication of Hunter's memoir in which he denied these allegations and the sale of his paintings kept the issue alive and prompted Republican criticisms even after Biden took office.

Anticipated Confirmation Problems

With control of the Senate in doubt until the outcome of the two special elections in Georgia held on January 5, 2021, the president-elect's senior advisors who made appointment recommendations to Biden were forced to anticipate possible Senate actions. Several candidates for top government positions were not nominated for fear of rejection.

To avoid the confirmation delays that marred the beginning of the Trump administration, the president-elect also designated acting secretaries, primarily senior civil servants, to serve until Biden's nominees to head the department or agency had been confirmed.

The transition staff created a special team to handle confirmations. Their initial task was to alert the bipartisan leaders of the Senate, committee chairs and other members who would consider the nomination, and senators from the nominee's home state, all before the president-elect went public with his selection. After the announcement of the prospective nominee, the congressional transition team mounted a public relations campaign in which they had cabinet-designate nominees tell their stories, meet with relevant interest group leaders, and be available for media interviews. Their credentials were amplified on social media by the transition staff.[14] The confirmation team ran into trouble when they did not involve key senators, take their past positions into account, or adequately brief them on the president's choices.

After the electors voted on December 14, 2020, Biden conducted a behind-the-scenes effort to communicate with Republican senators he knew who publicly or privately acknowledged him as the legitimate president-elect. He also engaged former department secretaries as well as a former Senate majority leader to help him with the confirmations.

Not only did Biden face potential partisan opposition, he had to consider Democratic opinion as well. Senator Ron Wyden (OR) publicly stated his disapproval of a candidate to run the Central Intelligence Agency on the grounds that the candidate had condoned the enhanced interrogation methods of the George W. Bush administration. In another case, the leading Democrat on the committee charged with considering the appointment of the Secretary of Defense had stated in 2017 when the Senate voted to modify the seven-year rule that he objected to waiving the rule again as did others, both Democratic and Republican.

The outcome of the Georgia Senate races was critical to the confirmation process as well as later policy decisions. Key participants in the transition, including the president and vice president-elect, helped raise money for the Democratic candidates, spoke at rallies for them in the weeks and days before that election, and sent 50 experienced campaign operatives to that state to aid in mobilizing the Democratic vote.

Their efforts were successful, an outcome that had significant implications for the transition and for governing. It allowed Biden to nominate U.S. Court of Appeals judge Merrick Garland for Attorney General because he was now confident that he could replace Garland on the court with a Democrat. More importantly, the Democrats gained party control of the Senate and the committees charged with confirming the nominees.[15]

But there were also potential problems, such as increased expectations of policy success in Congress and stronger presidential influence on legislative actions. Progressive Democrats could push harder for their liberal policy agenda, which, in turn, would evoke more opposition from conservative Republicans. The news media would highlight stories that placed the president and his administration in the center of more political controversies.

Electoral Certification and Impeachment Politics

Biden was acknowledged as the winner of the presidential election on November 7, 2020. Recounts had been held in a number of states in which the vote was close (Georgia, Michigan, and Wisconsin), but they did not change the official results. The lawsuits filed by Republicans protesting the election results were unsuccessful. Still claiming that he had won the election by a landslide, Trump turned to Congress.

The U.S. Constitution requires that states certify their electoral vote on December 10th; the vote was to be officially announced by the

President of the Senate, before a joint session of Congress, on January 6, 2021. President Trump tried to persuade Vice President Mike Pence, as the presiding officer of the Senate, to reverse the results, but he refused to do so.

On the day that Congress met to count the certified electoral votes and announce the winner, Trump had called for a "Save America Rally" on the National Mall in which he and his surrogates urged protestors to march to the Capitol to stop Congress from certifying Biden as the winner. Thousands did, breaching the police barriers, breaking into the locked Capitol, damaging and vandalizing it, and forcing the Capitol's security officers to move members of Congress quickly to more secure locations. One Capitol police officer died during the violence, as did four rioters. Most of the general public, watching the news coverage, were aghast at the desecration of this symbol of American democracy. A majority of Americans blamed Trump for the riot. His approval ratings fell sharply.[16]

During the siege of the Capitol, the president was glued to television news; aides had difficulty reaching him and persuading him to order the National Guard and to assemble them around the Capitol to help quell the riot. Vice President Pence had to do so. Later in the day, Trump issued a tweet asking supporters to be peaceful but continued to claim that the election had been stolen. Twitter later closed his account. The White House also released a short video of the president asking people to go home, a video that the president said privately he regretted making.

The riots had serious implications for the transfer of power but not the election outcome. Democrats and some Republicans wanted Trump to leave office immediately, hopefully by resigning, but if not, by invoking the 25th Amendment or by impeaching him. With 11 days before the inauguration, two of Trump's cabinet members resigned in protest; some Republicans condemned the violence; and Democrats urged his removal by impeachment.

Biden initially opposed impeaching Trump, fearing that it might fail in the Senate, would delay the confirmation of his nominees, and would divert attention from his actions in the presidency to Trump's response to the insurrection. He also did not want to inflame partisanship in Congress and the country as he was preaching unity.

Nonetheless, the president-elect deferred to Democratic congressional leaders, who in turn responded to demands from their members and the public to impeach the president for initiating and fueling the riot. A resolution was enacted by the House of Representatives on January 13,

2021, with all the Democrats and ten Republicans voting to impeach the president for incitement of insurrection. The Article of Impeachment, however, was not sent to the Senate immediately. Speaker Nancy Pelosi and Majority Leader Charles E. Schumer conferred on the most appropriate date for the Senate to receive it, which was more than a week later, January 25th. The Senate then delayed the trial for two weeks to allow Trump's attorneys to prepare his defense, a delay that allowed the confirmation process to continue.

Staffing for the White House and Cabinet

There are approximately 4,000 political appointments for a newly elected president to make; 1,200 of them require Senate consent, which includes over 800 of the top White House and Executive Office officials.[17]

Biden selected his top White House aides within the first week following his electoral victory; he continued to select personnel through his transition. By the end of 2020, he had chosen 49 senior aides and 51 others to work in the White House. A majority were women and people of color. About 20 percent were first-generation Americans. By the end of the transition, the number of senior presidential aides had increased, and the total White House staff numbered 251.

His national security office had the largest staff (35) followed by the president's counsel's office (22). The First Lady's staff had 16, the vice president's 14. Forty staffers worked on communications, digital strategy, and with the press. (See Table 2.1 for the heads of the principal offices in the first Biden White House.)

Biden also chose designated others to serve in the Executive Office of the President. Those who required Senate confirmation included the Chair of the Council of Economic Advisors, the Director of the OMB, the Controller of the Office of Federal Financial Management, the Chair of the Council of Environmental Quality, the U.S. Trade Representative, the Chief Agricultural Negotiator, the Director of the Office of Drug Control Policy, and the Director of the Office of Science, Technology, and Policy.

The top officials were a diverse group. For the 15 executive departments and nine other top-level cabinet positions, Biden nominated 13 men and 11 women. Of these nominees, six were African Americans, four Hispanic, three Asian American, and one Native American. Of those who identified their religious affiliation, eight were Catholic, five Jewish, three Protestant, and one Hindu. No White evangelicals or Muslims were included in the initial selections.

TABLE 2.1 Senior Appointees in the First Biden White House

First Lady	President	Vice President
Jill Biden	*Joe Biden*	*Kamala Harris*
Senior Advisors and Counselors	**Chief of Staff (COS)** *Ron Klain*	**Covid-19 Advisor** *Jeffrey Zients* ^
Mike Donilon *Anita Dunn* *Steve Ricchetti*	**Deputy COS** *Jen O'Malley Dillon*	**Deputy COS** *Bruce Reed/Neera Tanden**
Outreach Offices **Communications** *Kate Bedingfield*	**White House Operations** **Cabinet Secretary** *Evan Ryan*	**Policy Offices** **Domestic Climate** *Gina McCarthy*
	Counsel *Dana Remus*	
Digital Strategy *Rob Flaherty*	**Management and Administration** *Anne Filipic*	**Domestic Policy** *Susan Rice*
Intergovernmental Affairs *Julie Chavez Rodriquez*	**Oval Office Operations** *Annie Tomasini*	**Economic** *Brian Deese*
Legislative Affairs *Louisa Terrell*	**Personnel** *Catherine Russell*	**Homeland Security** *Elizabeth Sherwood-Randall*
Political Strategy and Outreach *Emmy Ruiz*	**Scheduling and Advance** *Ryan Montoya*	**National Security** *Jake Sullivan*
Press Secretary *Jen Psaki*	**Staff Secretary** *Jessica Hertz/Neera Tanden*	**Science Policy** *Eric Lander*
Public Engagement *Cedric Richmond*	**Social Secretary** *Carlos Elizondo*	
	Speech Writing *Vinay Reddy*	

*Appointed in mid-May after withdrawing her nomination as Director of the Office of Management and Budget; also became staff secretary in mid-October when Jessica Hertz resigned.

^ Also considered a senior advisor.

Previous public service was a major criterion for Biden. Fifteen cabinet-level appointees had served in the Obama administration; six of them worked in the Clinton administration. Biden believed that judgmental and administrative skills were of higher priority for his department secretaries than substantive policy expertise.

Questions were raised about some of the appointees. Denis McDonough, designated to be Secretary of Veteran Affairs, had not been in the military, although he had served on Obama's national security council and as his chief of staff. Xavier Becerra, Health and Human Services, had been a former member of Congress and had played a major role in the formulation, enactment, and later legal defense of the *Affordable Care Act*, but he was not a medical doctor or a health-care expert.[18] Also pro-choice, he was a target of pro-life groups. Republicans not only objected to his liberal views, but to the multistate lawsuits he initiated as California's Attorney General against the policies and actions of the Trump administration. Pete Buttigieg's knowledge of transportation issues, Merrick Garland's lack of prosecutorial experience, and General Lloyd Austin's 43 years of active Army duty also raised some concerns.

Comparative Capsule 2.1   Differences in Transition

BIDEN	TRUMP
Overcame delayed and politicized interactions	Fired director of transition
Most of the transition was conducted virtually	Had standard transition operations
Selected experienced public officials for White House and cabinet-level positions	Selected private sector CEOs and military officials for White House and cabinet-level positions

Notes

1. "Center for Presidential Transition," *Partnership for Public Service*, https://www.gsa.gov/about-us/mission-and-background/gsas-role-in-presidential-transitions, accessed December 6, 2020.
2. The Clinton to Bush transition, however, was marred by acts of vandalism and destruction in the White House and Executive Office Building, allegedly by employees who supported Al Gore. The General Accounting Office estimated the cost of the damage to be between $13,000 and $14,000.
3. Bob Woodward and Roberta Costa, *Peril* (New York: Simon and Schuster, 2021).
4. Paul Kane and Scott Clement, "220 GOP Lawmakers Silent on Biden Victory," *Washington Post*, December 6, 2020.
5. Amber Phillips, "The 5-Minute Fix," *Washington Post*, November 16, 2020.
6. The president-elect and vice president-elect did not get their first intelligence briefings until November 29th, almost four weeks after the election.
7. The most controversial of these Trump appointees was Richard Ellis, a former Republican congressional aide, who was made the top lawyer of the National Security Agency, giving him access to large amounts of classified information. The head

of the agency opposed the appointment but was overruled by the Acting Secretary of Defense. Democrats were furious about the appointment, with the Speaker of the House demanding that Ellis be terminated. Lisa Rein and Anne Gearan, "Biden May Be Stuck With Some Trump Loyalists," *Washington Post*, January 26, 2021.

8. "The 2020–21 Presidential Transition," *The Partnership for Public Service*, January 20, 2022.

9. Annie Linskey and Ashley Parker, "Biden Aims to Restore Order After Four Years of Tumult," *Washington Post*, January 24, 2021.

10. In his first year alone, more than one-third of Trump's top political appointees in the White House and Executive Office of the President left and were replaced, often several times. Kathryn Gunn Tenpas, "Tracking Turnover in the Trump Administration," *Brookings Institution*, December, 2020.

11. Kathryn Gunn Tenpas, "Tracking Turnover in the Trump Administration," *Brookings Institution*, December, 2020.

12. "Public Sees Wealthy People, Corporations Growing Influence in Trump Era," *Pew Research Center*, January 18, 2017; "Trust and Distrust in America," *Pew Research Center*, July 22, 2019.

13. Neera Tanden's nomination as OMB's director was the most controversial because of partisan tweets she had written during the Trump presidency that were critical of Republican officials in government. The Biden administration's failure to contact, much less ascertain, the extent of the opposition to her nomination by Republican Senators and one Democrat contributed to her difficulties, and finally her nomination was withdrawn when it was clear she would not get the votes needed to be confirmed.

14. Katasha Korecki and Christopher Cadelago, "Amid a Crisis Like 'We've Never Seen,' Biden Drives to Fill Cabinet," *Politico*, December 21, 2020.

15. The first hearings, however, for top national security positions were held the day before the Inauguration with the Republicans still nominally in control of the Senate.

16. "Biden Begins Presidency With Positive Ratings; Trump Departs With Lowest-Ever Job Mark," *Pew Research Center*, January 15, 2021.

17. Ballotpedia's *Transition Tracker*, January 5, 2021.

18. Becerra's wife is a doctor.

PART II

THE FIRST 100 DAYS

Biden's first ten days in office were well planned, well organized, and well executed. There was little spontaneity, little controversy, and considerable news coverage.

The Inauguration

President Biden's inauguration departed from traditional ones because of the pandemic and security concerns that followed the Capitol insurrection of January 6. The ceremonial part of the day, the prayers, oaths, and formalities, were conducted with suitable pomp; many were conducted virtually. Inauguration attendance was limited to about 1,000. People were urged to watch the events at home.

All the participants were masked (except when speaking), the parade was canceled, and the 400,000 Americans who died from the virus were mourned at Arlington National Cemetery. Twenty-five thousand soldiers from the National Guard and many others from federal law enforcement agencies were on hand to prevent violence.

The president's 21-minute address was a plea for unity and community, fellowship and civility, dialogue not diatribes. Only together, Biden argued, could the country conquer the problems it faced in the winter of 2021. "To overcome these challenges—to restore the soul and to secure the future of America—requires more than words. It requires the most elusive of things in a democracy: unity. unity."[1] Biden sought to pacify, not arouse; he promised to serve the public good, not his own self-interests.

The president's sober tone and hopeful words contrasted sharply with his predecessor four years earlier, as did the imagery of the inauguration itself.

DOI: 10.4324/9781003176978-5

Photo 3.1 *Biden gives his inaugural address to a socially distanced audience in January 2021*
Source: Tasos Katopodis/Pool Photo via AP Photo

The speech, well received by those in attendance and most of the news commentators, was followed by a memorial service at Arlington National Cemetery, also with words of unity and support for the president from three of his four immediate predecessors, Bill Clinton, George W. Bush, and Barack Obama. Donald Trump did not attend the inauguration, nor did 96-year-old Jimmy Carter, who was too frail to travel to Washington.

The President's Schedule and Actions

In an effort to deal with the problems that confronted the country as quickly as possible, the Biden team used Franklin Roosevelt's first days as its model. Speeches and activities were carefully scripted, well-orchestrated, and fast paced. The president's executive actions and legislative initiatives were designed to indicate the return to competent, substantive, and crises-driven leadership.

Policy priorities had been designated for each workday and given to the news media by Biden's designated chief of staff, Ron Klain. (See Box 3.1.)

Box 3.1 Biden's Policy Objectives

The Pandemic

- set up a COVID-19 office in the White House, reporting directly to the president;
- require masks on federal property;
- rejoin the World Health Organization.

The Economy

- delay student debt collection;
- extend the moratoriums on evictions and foreclosures;
- ban employment discrimination against LGBTQ workers.

The Environment

- rejoin the Paris Climate Accords;
- revoke the permit for the Keystone Pipeline and others for fossil fuel extraction from U.S. lands.

Immigration

- count all immigrants, legal and illegal, in the census;
- provide legal status for those individuals, "Dreamers," included in the Deferred Action for Childhood Arrivals plan;
- revise procedures for enforcing immigration laws;
- enhance border security with technology; stop construction of the wall along the Mexican border;
- eliminate the ban on travel from several Muslim countries; extend deportation protections for Liberians.

Government

- broaden the ethics pledge for government employees;[2]
- review all regulations issued during the last days of the Trump administration;

> - revise the process by which regulations were evaluated by the Office of Management and Budget (OMB) and issued by the agencies.
>
> *Source*: Ron Klain, "Memo to the President," Biden-Harris Transition Team, January 16, 2021.

Comparative Capsule 3.1   First Days

BIDEN	TRUMP
Inaugural theme: "Unity, Unity"	Inaugural theme: "Make America Great Again"
Devoted each full working day to another major priority	Repeal Obama's liberal agenda and promote his own
Meet public expectations on how a president should look, act, and behave	Demonstrate strong personal presidential leadership
Appoint knowledgeable and experienced public officials	Appoint innovative, experienced, and successful private sector CEOs

Implementing the Game Plan

A principal goal of the first ten days of presidential activities was to demonstrate a routinized White House and a predictable president in contrast to the chaos of the Trump White House. Back to normal was the message, imagery, and mode of operation of the Biden White House.

January 20—Day 1

Biden began the work portion of Inauguration Day at 5:30 p.m. in the White House, signing 17 executive orders, memorandums, and proclamations. He also proposed two major legislative initiatives. The day ended with a two-hour national showcase of talent across the country, hosted by Tom Hanks, and watched by Biden and millions of Americans. The new president also gave his grandchildren a tour of the White House.

January 21—Day 2

On his first full workday, 9 a.m. to about 7 p.m., the president dealt with the pandemic by announcing that the administration would increase the amount of data on COVID-19 and provide more equipment, testing, and vaccinations to cope with it. Biden's initial goal was to vaccinate 100 million Americans within his first 100 days in office. He evoked the *Defense Production Act* to facilitate the efforts to do so. He also issued a mask-wearing requirement for interstate travel as well as eight additional executive orders, memos, and department directives that established a Pandemic Testing Board, a Health Equity Task Force, and guidelines for opening schools and keeping workers safe. He pledged to support international efforts to fight the disease.

In addition to focusing on the health crisis, the president fired the general counsel of the National Labor Relations Board (NLRB), a Trump appointee, when he refused to resign,[3] and answered congratulatory calls from foreign leaders, including the prime minister of Canada and the president of Mexico. Short summaries of these conversations were released to the news media and posted on the White House's website.

January 22—Day 3

The next day's focus on economic relief began with a presidential order to the Departments of Agriculture, Labor, Treasury, and Veterans Affairs to help the needy during the health and economic crises by distributing stimulus checks faster, expanding food assistance programs, delaying debt collection for military families, and enabling employees who refused to work in unsafe conditions to remain eligible for unemployment benefits.

In his effort to restore the reputation and operational efficiency of the executive branch, Biden reversed Trump's efforts to politicize the upper echelons of the civil service, reduce collective bargaining rights of federal unions, and disregard diversity in hiring and training. He saw these actions as a first step to revitalize the merit-based civil service system, boost career employees' morale, fill hundreds of vacancies left by Trump, generate greater job security, promote diversity, and rebuild public confidence in government. Agencies were asked to conduct background checks on Trump's late appointees to civil service positions, assess their job performance, and determine whether any of the political conversions to career status violated the merit-based system or prevented promotions of deserving government employees.

Some of Trump appointees who were transferred into the civil service protested their removal; some claimed reverse partisan discrimination. Nonetheless, the new administration proceeded to request the resignations of most of Trump's political appointees, including those on non-paying boards and commissions. Officials who refused to do so were sent emails terminating their service, closing their email accounts, voiding their government-issued credit cards, and removing their names from department and agency websites. In some cases, entire boards, councils, and commissions were eliminated entirely.[4]

The president also promised regulatory reform and asked the OMB and department heads to review all regulations and not issue new ones until the review was completed. The objective was to reverse Trump's executive actions to which the administration and its Democratic supporters strongly objected. Republicans criticized the review and feared it would encourage the government to issue more new and restrictive regulations on private individuals and companies.[5]

January 23 and 24—Days 4 and 5

No public events were scheduled for the first weekend, although on Saturday, the president met with his key health and economic advisors. On Sunday, he attended Mass in Georgetown, forecasting the routine he planned to follow on Saturdays, Sundays, and some holidays. Biden normally relaxed at home or at Camp David with his wife, family, and friends. As a devout Catholic, he attended church regularly, a practice his predecessor did not follow. He also played golf with family and friends, but not to the extent that Trump did.

January 25—Day 6

The president announced his *Buy American* program on the Monday following his first weekend in office. He ordered the government to give preference to purchasing products made in America. Since many parts of these products were purchased from abroad, Biden reduced the percentage and value of foreign components to qualify the product as American. The president also banned travel to the United States from countries infected with new variants of the coronavirus, including Brazil and most of Europe, and reversed his predecessor's prohibition of transgender individuals serving in the military.

January 27—Day 7

Equity was the daily theme. The president created a commission on policing, ordered the Justice Department to eliminate the use of private prisons, and pledged the improvement of federal prisons; he sought to combat racism against Asian Americans, directed agencies to consult with tribal leaders, and asked the Department of Housing and Urban Development to examine and eliminate discrimination in housing. The administration also announced a 16 percent increase in the federal government's distribution of the coronavirus vaccine and new procedures for moving it quickly to the states.

January 28—Day 8

The White House focused on immigration issues. The president expanded the resettlement of refugees in the United States and ordered that minors, separated from their families at the border, be reunited with their parents or relatives, or if that were not possible, placed with foster parents or social organizations that would cater to their needs. He also halted deportation of illegal immigrants for 100 days, an order that was challenged by a Texas lawsuit and temporarily halted by a federal judge.

January 29—Day 9

The White House highlighted science and climate change. The president set up a council of advisors for science and technology, terminated the permit for the Keystone Pipeline, and announced that his administration would review all leasing on federal lands and waters for the purpose of extracting fossil fuels.

January 30—Day 10

Directing his attention to health care, the president reopened the enrollment period for the Affordable Care Act and Medicaid for three additional months and lifted restrictions on international funding to nongovernmental groups that provided abortion information or services.

In summary, the first ten days imposed Biden's stamp on the presidency. He issued twenty five executive orders, ten memorandums, two directives, and four proclamations compared to Trump's six executive orders, seven memorandums, and two proclamations during the same period of time. Trump, however, also approved sixteen congressional actions under the *Congressional Review Act* that revoked rules and orders that were issued by Obama during the last 60 days of his presidency.

Biden's extensive executive activity generated allegations from Republicans that he was governing by decree, to which he replied: "There's a lot of talk with good reason about the number of executive orders I've signed. I'm not making new law. I'm eliminating bad policy."[6]

Operational Style

The White House

The president's standard practice was to arrive at the Oval Office around 9 a.m.; White House aides came earlier. An intelligence briefing initiated presidential activities in which he and usually the vice president attended. After the briefing, the president would announce his executive actions and legislative proposals with his communications office providing summaries and fact sheets that were posted on the White House website. After lunch, the president or one of his senior staff or policy experts would give brief remarks followed by a "gaggle" with reporters, which Press Secretary Jen Psaki held. Sometimes, she would invite experts in the particular policy area under discussion to join her. Senior officials and department secretaries would also be made available to the news media when the White House believed that they could provide details that influenced news media coverage.

The overall objective of these White House operations was to demonstrate institutional continuity and message consistency in contrast to Trump's less predictable remarks and actions and his tweet-driven communications. Most of Biden's planned statements and policy decisions had been previously discussed by policy experts and senior presidential aides, with the president participating in the final stages of the decision-making process. The president's executive actions had also been scrutinized by White House lawyers to ensure that they did not exceed the constitutional and statutory limits of his authority.

The President

Biden's personal style—calm, determined, resolute but flexible, a trustworthy person who made sound policy judgments—contrasted sharply with Trump's manner and more instinctive decision-making. Biden wanted to meet generic expectations of the rhetoric a president should use and how he should work and behave within public view.

Biden stuck to the script that was mounted on teleprompters to discourage his often noted tendency to meander and make off-the-cuff remarks. His remarks tended to be short and directed to the topic at hand.

Initial Communications Strategy

Another objective of the Biden White House was to control the news media's agenda. Unlike Trump, Biden held no interviews with reporters in his first two weeks. Designated cabinet secretaries, however, appeared regularly on the news shows with the White House orchestrating their appearances and prepping their comments. Representatives of outside groups, interested and involved in the president's policy agenda, were invited to meet with the president and his senior advisors virtually or, occasionally, in person. Initially, the White House refused to release the names of those who attended virtual sessions with high-ranking officials and the president and vice president, but eventually the administration was pressured to publicize the names of those who actually visited White House offices, but not the president's residence.

The president made one joint address to Congress near the end of his first 100 days in which he lauded his administration's accomplishments, discussed the issues that lay ahead, indicated plans for dealing with them, and praised Americans for their continuing support in a speech seen by about 27 million households. Most of the viewers were age 55 years and older.[7]

Biden also had a digital strategy group that wrote almost all the initial tweets that appeared on @POTUS. They were primarily promotional and not nearly as newsworthy as Trump's. Biden did not tweet very much himself, but his chief of staff tweeted a lot.[8]

Executive Actions and Legislative Initiatives

Although the president continued to issue executive orders and memorandums, he could not achieve desired policy changes by them alone. With the exception of proclamations, most of which are hortatory, executive orders, memos, and directives apply only to executive branch employees, not the general public. Orders can be modified or reversed by a president, usually one from a different party, voided by Congress, altered by legislation, or challenged on constitutional grounds in the judiciary.

Nominations

Before taking office, Biden readied 23 nominations of top-level cabinet officials; however, the Senate was slow to consider them. Not until the dispute over the election outcome, the special elections in Georgia, and the power-sharing agreement between the majority and minority leaders were resolved did the committees tasked with considering the nominees begin the process. The Trump impeachment trial also slowed the Senate. It took over two months to confirm all the department secretaries in the executive branch, which forced the White House to coordinate many of its initiatives, such as its COVID-19 response, itself. Confirmation delays plagued previous administrations as well.[9]

Legislation

During Biden's first week in office, only one legislative act had been enacted into law, the seven-year waiver to permit General Lloyd Austin to become Secretary of Defense. The bill was opposed by 78 members of the House and 27 senators who cited civilian control of the military as the primary reason for their opposition.

The president proposed two major legislative initiatives on his first full day in office, one on the pandemic and economic relief and the other on immigration reform. Both proposals encountered stiff opposition, primarily but not exclusively from Republicans. The bipartisan approach that the president initially pursued took time, required compromise, and was opposed by partisan activists of both parties. Republicans complained that Biden's quest for unity was all talk and no substance, that his administration had not reached out to them on these major legislative matters, that the president had not appointed a Republican to his cabinet, and that he had used executive authority far more than his predecessor. Progressive Democrats, on the other hand, were impatient and did not want to dilute their policy priorities with bipartisan political compromises.

Biden initially deferred to Democratic leaders in both houses of Congress to coordinate input and support for his stimulus legislation. When Republicans protested his reliance on a partisan majority, Biden narrowed his definition of unity, saying: "If you pass a piece of legislation that breaks down on party lines, but it gets passed, it doesn't mean there wasn't unity, it just means it wasn't bipartisan."[10]

The options the president faced reflected the political environment he had inherited, an environment that had not changed materially since the 2020 election, with the partisan divide as deep and wide as ever. Combined with the separation of powers, the polarization of the parties, factions within them, and the absence of a consensus of how to deal with the country's most important problems, the president's legislative road ahead would be tough and tedious.

Notes

1. President Joe Biden's Inaugural Address, January 20, 2021, *White House*.
2. The new code of conduct for executive officials that prohibited them from accepting gifts from lobbyists and from working on matters they had dealt with in their private sector employment for a period of two years. A two-year limit was reestablished to preclude officials who left the administration from lobbying their former agencies and the White House. On his last morning as president, Trump had removed the restriction he had placed on his appointees from lobbying the agencies in which they worked, thereby reopening the swamp he promised to drain.
3. The firing was controversial. The NLRB was considered an independent agency in which appointees served a designated period of time. The employee dismissed by Biden claimed he refused to resign because he had ten more months in which to serve.
4. Secretary of Defense Austin abolished 42 boards that advised the department on his first days in office.
5. Erin Hawley, "The Biden Administration's New Regulation Superweapon," *National Review*, February 8, 2021.
6. Joe Biden, "Remarks by President Biden at Signing of Executive Orders," *White House*, February 2, 2021.
7. Brian Stelter, "Biden's First Address to Congress Wasn't Immune to TV Ratings Erosion," *CNN*, April 29, 2021.
8. Alex Thompson and Theodoric Meyer, "Transition Playbook," *Politico*, January 26, 2021.
9. Obama and Trump did not gain confirmation of all of their cabinet secretaries until one month later.
10. Philip Bump, "Biden Just Set a Very High Bar for When He Thinks He Will Have Achieved Unity," *Washington Post*, January 25, 2021.

CHAPTER 4

CONTEMPORARY DOMESTIC POLITICS AND POLICYMAKING

The President's Limited Political Resources

The Biden presidency had to operate in a fractious political environment in Congress and the country, and the president had to repair a government that had lost the confidence and trust of the American people.[1] Only 27 percent of the public indicated that they were satisfied with the system of government and how well it was working when he took office.[2] To improve perceptions of government, Biden needed leadership skills and more political resources to deal with Congress successfully and achieve his legislative goals.

At the outset, however, he did not have those resources, and his leadership skills as president were untested. Biden did not achieve as overwhelming an electoral victory as Obama or the partisan advantage that his Democratic predecessor had upon taking office, 256 House Democrats and 56 Senate Democrats plus two Independents who caucused with this party. Even with a significant political majority in Congress, only one legislative act had been passed during Obama's first month, the *Lilly Ledbetter Fair Pay Act*, which George W. Bush had twice vetoed.

Obama also lost a critical first month by trying unsuccessfully to gain Republican backing for legislation to combat the steep economic recession. As a consequence, Democrats had to use a reconciliation process that required a simple majority to enact the *American Recovery and Reinvestment Act*. The delay in enacting the legislation and Obama's failure to promote the new law encouraged former Obama officials who joined the Biden administration to move quickly to achieve and publicize their first major legislative accomplishment.

Trump also began his presidency with his party in control of Congress, but unlike Obama, he did not win a majority of the 2016 popular

DOI: 10.4324/9781003176978-6

vote or have to contend with a major economic crisis. That Trump ridiculed the establishment, including Republicans, got him off to a rocky start with Congress. He failed to achieve his first legislative goal to repeal and replace the *Affordable Care Act* (Obamacare). It was May before the Republican Congress enacted its first major legislation, a consolidated appropriations bill.

Biden had fewer congressional assets than the two presidents that preceded him: he had a smaller partisan majority in the House, an evenly divided Senate, an election victory without presidential coattails, and one that continued to be disputed by his opponent, including most Republican members of Congress. Biden was also burdened with a large increase in the national debt that occurred during the previous four years, multiple and costly medical challenges to control the pandemic and revive the economy, and an impatient public that wanted the crises ended.

The president needed legislation: the problems could not be solved by executive actions alone. Complicating the early achievement of Biden's legislative policy goals in a polarized Senate was a full calendar that included confirmation of his new appointees and the pending impeachment of Donald Trump. When Senator Rand Paul (KY) introduced a procedural resolution that objected to impeaching a president no longer in office, all but five Republican senators voted in favor of it. Many of them had objected to Trump's speech and inactions on January 6, 2021, but feared that the day of the Capitol Hill insurrection would be remembered by candidates who faced reelection and feared retribution from him and a majority of his electoral base.[3] The vote indicated that the enactment of legislation needing 60 votes in the Senate to pass was unlikely.

Partisan Politics and Policies

From the day Biden took office, partisan divisions within and between the two major parties affected legislation, White House statements and actions, and news coverage and commentary. There was even speculation about the formation of a third party by or against Trump. A majority of the public (62 percent) favored the idea of another party, but establishment politicians opposed it, especially Trump.[4]

Nonetheless, both Democrats and Republicans looked ahead to the midterm elections as a means for expanding their political coalitions and extending their influence in Congress and state and local governments.

Biden decided to deposit funds left over from his campaign, or raised in the future, into the Democratic National Committee (DNC) account for use in the midterm elections. This decision contrasted with the practices of former Presidents Obama and Trump, who kept their political organizations and war chests intact for their own future use. Biden hoped his plan would extend his influence with elected Democrats and reverse or reduce the traditional loss of seats that the party controlling the White House usually suffers in its first midterm election.

Internal party politics persisted throughout 2021. Progressive Democrats pressured the administration to adhere to Biden's campaign promises and to their liberal policy agenda. The progressives railed against the Senate's filibuster rule but lacked the votes to overturn it. Biden initially opposed changing the rule as well. As a consequence, progressive Democrats planned to use the reconciliation process that required only a simple majority vote in the Senate to achieve their policy goals.

Mitch McConnell, the Senate Minority Leader, promised to follow the practices he had pursued during the last six years of the Obama administration to thwart the enactment of legislation that he and most other GOP senators opposed. Although Republican members of Congress gave lip service to Trump as party leader, their voting behavior was more influenced by their elected congressional party leaders.

Impeachment

In the midst of consideration of deliberating on proposals to help Americans survive the pandemic and economic downturn, the House of Representatives voted to send one Article of Impeachment to the Senate, charging Trump with inciting the January 6 Capitol riot. Although the Constitution requires the upper chamber to begin the impeachment trial immediately and suspend other business, the trial was scheduled on February 9th to give Trump's attorneys two weeks to prepare his defense.

Biden initially chose to stay out of the fray, claiming impeachment was a congressional responsibility, not a presidential one. His press secretary reiterated the president's intention, describing Biden as president, not a political pundit. During the trial, however, which was covered live on cable news networks, Biden conceded that he had watched clips of the riots that the Democratic impeachment managers had presented to the Senate and surmised that the video evidence could change the opinions of some Republicans.

Throughout the five days of the trial, the president and his aides busied themselves with White House matters and projected an image of normal operations. Although Democrats knew the likely outcome of the impeachment vote, they wanted to remind the general public about Trump's seditious behavior, incendiary remarks, and unsupported claims that the 2020 election was rigged. They also wanted to spotlight Senate Republicans who voted to acquit the president to diminish their chances for reelection.

Republicans understandably were unhappy about the trial and tried to divert attention from Trump's election fraud allegations and his behavior during the Capitol insurrection. Many of them also wanted to reduce Trump's influence within the party but could not say so in public. Both sides agreed, however, that they wanted Trump off the front page after the trial was over.

The Democratic impeachment managers spent two days presenting visual and written testimony, arguing that Trump committed an impeachable offense as president. Trump's lawyers responded that it was unconstitutional to impeach an ex-president. They also defended him on the grounds of freedom of speech and failure to prove that his speech at the rally and previous remarks on the election incited the riot.

Although few Senate Republicans defended Trump, only ten voted alongside all 48 Democrats and two Independents to convict him, seven votes short of the two-thirds Senate majority necessary to do so. Before and again after the trial, a slight majority of Americans favored impeaching the president.[5] Had Trump been convicted, and the Senate followed its past practices, that body could also have prevented him from holding elected office again by a simple majority vote.

After the Senate voted, Biden issued a statement that condemned the violence and supported democratic values, but did not mention Trump by name. He said:

> This sad chapter in our history has reminded us that democracy is fragile. That it must always be defended. That we must be ever vigilant. That violence and extremism has no place in America. And that each of us has a duty and responsibility as Americans, and especially as leaders, to defend the truth and to defeat the lies.[6]

With the impeachment over, the president continued his efforts to build support for his rescue plan. He participated in a CNN-sponsored town meeting in Wisconsin followed by a visit to a Pfizer vaccine facility in Michigan and a trip to Texas to inspect the damage caused by a fierce winter storm. His days of White House confinement were over by mid-February.

The American Rescue Plan

Biden's initial legislative proposal for the pandemic and economic recovery was large, comprehensive, and costly. It included a government grant of $1,400 for low-income individuals, an increase in the child tax credit, funds for state and local governments, unemployment insurance, and more money for reopening schools, testing for the virus, distributing vaccines, and giving loans for small businesses, childcare, and rental assistance. His original plan also contained an increase in the national minimum wage to $15 an hour. The total price tag for the proposal was $1.9 trillion.

Republicans objected to the high cost and some of the provisions (minimum wage, state and local aid, and the level of income eligibility), pointing out that a $900 billion bill had been enacted in December 2020, the last month of the Trump presidency, and some money from that bill still had not been spent. A few Democrats were also concerned about the size of the stimulus checks and the income levels at which people would receive them.

In pushing the legislation, the president's aides emphasized that the public supported most of its contents, especially the stimulus checks and COVID-19 funding. The White House campaigned for the legislation by gaining endorsements from elected officials, economists, interest group leaders, and a bipartisan group of 400 mayors.[7] Senior presidential advisors participated in more than 100 television, radio, and podcast interviews.[8] At a town meeting in mid-February, Biden reiterated the primacy of the COVID-19 issue and his administration's efforts to increase the supply and improve the distribution of the vaccine; by July, he said there would be sufficient amounts to vaccinate every American. Polls indicated that the public was supportive of the administration's COVID-19 response by an almost two to one margin (59 percent approval, 31 percent disapproval).[9]

Although many Senate Republicans declared the proposal dead on arrival, ten of them met with the president to propose a less costly alternative totaling $618 billion. Their plan included a smaller stimulus given to fewer people and a smaller extension of unemployment insurance, but no diminishment in virus funding. They wanted to consider the size of the national minimum wage separately, not in Biden's bill.

The issue for the president was compromise versus speed. Democrats preferred the latter, desiring to move quickly to contain and reverse the pandemic and to jump-start the economy. Biden sided with his party. He indicated that he was flexible on the income level necessary to receive the stimulus but not on the amount of the stimulus itself, $1,400. Children born in the United States would be eligible for child support even if their parents were in the country illegally. Biden also wanted quick action that required the use of the reconciliation process. Once the Democrats were certain that they had the votes, they introduced budget resolutions that were passed in both chambers, with Vice President Harris casting the tie-breaking vote in the Senate.

The original Biden proposal suffered two casualties in the bill that was enacted into law, the absence of a minimum wage increase that the Senate Parliamentarian ruled could not be included in the reconciliation bill and a decrease in the amount and extension of additional unemployment benefits, which Senator Joe Manchin (D-WV) opposed.

The American Rescue Plan Act of 2021 was a major victory for the president. Biden made his first prime-time speech the day after it became law, promising to make vaccines available to everyone over the age of 16 years by the first of May. He subsequently did so by mid-April. He also indicated that by July 4th, social get-togethers with family and friends would be possible. Gene Sperling, who had served in the Obama administration, was chosen to oversee implementation of the legislation.

The week after the bill was signed into law, the president, vice president, First Lady, and Second Gentleman initiated a public relations campaign to explain and praise the plan. The White House organized a COVID-19 Community Corps, composed of health experts and community leaders. Polls indicated that the vaccination campaign was working.[10]

Opposition came from anti-vaccine groups. Much of it was generated by supporters of Trump, even though he had gotten a shot and urged others to do so. One-third of Republicans indicated that they would not get vaccinated, compared to 10 percent of Democrats and 23 percent of Independents.[11] By the end of February, those percentages began to decline; by the end of the president's first 100 days, 145 million Americans (43.3 percent) received at least one dose of the Pfizer or Moderna vaccines, and more than 100 million got the prescribed two doses (30 percent). More than 300 million doses had been distributed by the government.[12]

Immigration Dilemmas

Immigration reform, another major priority of the Biden administration, posed a host of political problems on which the country was divided, such as providing a path to citizenship for immigrants without legal status, expanding the number of asylum seekers admitted, and issuing green cards (work permits) and a shortened path to citizenship to minors brought into the country illegally but who grew up in the United States. Although a majority of Americans believed immigration was a good thing and had benefited the country, they also wanted secure borders, humane enforcement, and an end to the construction of a wall between Mexico and the United States.[13]

Publicly, the White House stood firmly behind its original goal; privately and later publicly, Biden indicated flexibility, such as dividing immigration reform into separate legislative measures in which bipartisan support was possible. Enhancing security at ports of entry, enacting legal status and a path to citizenship for "Dreamers," easing visa restrictions for seasonal workers, and providing undocumented workers in the United States with the possibility of becoming American citizens appeared to be subjects on which common ground might exist. Democratic sponsors of immigration reform took both tracks, proposing a comprehensive bill as well as more specific and limited proposals.

The political differences over immigration, however, also prompted the president to reverse Trump's orders that Democrats found most egregious: the construction of the border wall, denying entrance to the United States from several Muslim countries, and separating children from their parents. Biden ordered a 100-day pause on deportation while his administration reviewed enforcement procedures currently in place. His executive order halting construction engendered an immediate and successful legal challenge. The president also voided a national emergency declaration on immigration that permitted rapid deportation of illegal immigrants.[14]

The president introduced his immigration proposals to Congress in mid-February, and they were detailed in the *U.S. Citizenship Act of 2021*. The comprehensive legislation provided a path to citizenship for 11 million undocumented immigrants, expanded the number of visas, removed restrictions on family-based policies, gave legal status to "Dreamers" and essential workers, and allowed $400 billion in aid to the depressed economies in Central America to improve the conditions that prompted immigration to the United States.

The president's actions and his policy proposals triggered a flood of asylum seekers at the southern border, the most in 15 years: 100,000 in February; 170,000 in March; and more than 200,000 by the summer. Thousands of unaccompanied children sought entry. Although the Biden administration expanded deportations, the president refused to repatriate unaccompanied minors.

Customs and border agents were overwhelmed, detention facilities were overcrowded, and conditions in shelters deteriorated. The problems were magnified when the Mexican government reversed its policy of allowing asylum seekers, waiting at the border for their cases to come before U.S. immigration courts, to be sheltered in Mexico as had been done during Trump's presidency.

Biden decided initially to admit asylum seekers slowly and release minors who came alone within 72 hours as required by law to relatives, friends, or service organizations. This plan proved to be unworkable because of the very large number of immigrants seeking entry. Facing a fast-growing humanitarian problem, the Biden administration had to rent convention centers, use military bases and a former camp for oil workers as temporary shelters, and engage private sector companies to help in providing needed services.

The administration had another problem. Although the Secretary of the Department of Homeland Security who oversaw immigration matters had been confirmed, most of the key immigration agencies that administered services such as Customs and Border Protection, the Administration for Children and Families, Immigration and Customs Enforcement, and Citizenship and Immigrant Services did not have confirmed directors in charge, only acting ones who lacked the clout and connections to coordinate multiagency activities. Moreover, the chief border coordinator in the White House had announced her intention to leave at the end of Biden's first 100 days. It was not until mid-April that Biden began to nominate directors of these agencies.

The immigration court system contributed to the problem as well. It had a backlog of 1.3 million cases.[15] There was also the related issue of the judges themselves, most of whom had been appointed by the previous president and were not as sympathetic to the plight of asylum seekers as Biden.[16] Adding more immigration judges would have been expensive and time consuming, so the administration tasked some experienced customs and border security officials to make decisions on asylum cases as well.

The White House also initiated a public relations campaign aimed at Mexico and Central America to discourage immigration to the United States and provided financial aid to El Salvador, Guatemala, and Honduras to improve the conditions that prompted people to leave. Vice President Harris was put in charge of directing diplomatic negotiations with the leaders of those countries, which she initially did virtually, but she did not go to the border until Republican criticism exploded in the news media.

As the crisis grew worse, its public impact expanded. More than 70 percent of Americans perceived the flood of immigrants to be a major problem.[17] Biden's approval on handling the issue hovered in the low 40 percent range.[18] The immigration crisis led to a related problem for the president. It discouraged him from fulfilling a promise to allow more legal immigrants into the country. Pressure from pro-immigration groups and Democratic progressives, however, forced Biden to increase

Photo 4.1 *Vice President Kamala Harris tours the U.S. Customs and Border Protection Central Processing Center*
Source: *AP Photo/Jacquelyn Martin*

the number to 65,500 in the 2021 fiscal year and 125,000 for the next one. Trump had set a cap of 15,000, but the actual number to gain entry was even lower.[19]

Democratic lawmakers in the House of Representatives began to devise new legislation that they believed had the best chance of gaining some bipartisan support and sent two bills to the Senate in March—the *American Dream and Promise Act of 2021* and the *Farm Workforce Modernization Act.* The legislation provided legal status and a path to citizenship for children brought into the United States illegally, plus temporary legal status and an option to seek citizenship for migrant farm workers. In April, the House also enacted legislation to limit a president's power to issue travel bans as Trump had done, and to allow travelers with proper U.S. credentials (passports, visas, or green cards) to request a lawyer, relative, or friend if stopped by U.S. border authorities, but the Senate was too busy in the summer and fall of 2021 to consider these proposals.

Infrastructure Proposals

Biden introduced his infrastructure plan initiatives at the end of March. Calling it a jobs program that would result in economic revitalization and make the United States more competitive internationally, he claimed that it would expand the employment opportunities for the middle class. A vital component of the program dealt with climate change. Lead pipes and service lines for drinking water would be replaced, public transit improved and electrified, harmful gas emissions decreased, the power grid secured and upgraded, and more wind and solar energy projects would be incentivized by the government, all in addition to repairing roads, bridges, ports, and tunnels and, if need be, building new ones. Revitalizing technology manufacturing, such as semiconductors, creating a network of charging stations for electronic vehicles, and improving the structures and energy efficiency of housing were also included in his proposal.

Social issues, such as childcare and care for the elderly and the disabled, universal preschool education, free community colleges, grants for students at four-year colleges and universities, and extended family leave for workers were also included—the human dimension of the country's infrastructure.

The president believed these projects would increase opportunities for most Americans, particularly minorities, and give them the skills to compete in an increasingly technological society. The cost of these new programs would be met by increased corporate taxation rates, higher capital gains taxes, and a more progressive income tax on wealthy Americans. Biden also proposed to increase the size and scope of the Internal Revenue Service to recover billions in unpaid taxes.

Polls indicated public support for these projects. A majority of people favored the paid family leave, extending the deductions on childcare, and additional help for the elderly and disabled; more than two-thirds of those surveyed were in favor of safeguarding the internet, expanding broadband to rural areas, and improving public schools; and a majority of Americans even favored increasing corporate taxes to help generate additional revenue, although a majority of Republicans did not.[20]

Congressional Republicans were opposed, however, to the price tag of $2.25 trillion, expanding government's size and services, and stricter climate regulations. They also objected to raising taxes after their legislative enactment had lowered them.

Biden met with Republican members of Congress a number of times, in cordial but not productive sessions. The president indicated that he preferred a bipartisan bill but also said that delay was not an option in enacting it.

Defining infrastructure became a partisan issue. Biden defined it broadly to include physical and human dimensions; Republicans defined it narrowly to include only the physical aspects.

For the White House, the decision came down to seeking bipartisan support on parts of the plan or wrapping as much as possible into a reconciliation bill. Bipartisanship for congressional Democrats posed two major problems: getting the 60 votes needed for closure and reducing the climate and social programs. Reconciliation, on the other hand, required unified Democratic support in the Senate, nearly unified support in the House, and a series of favorable decisions by the Senate Parliamentarian on what could be included in a reconciliation bill. The debate on the scope and content of the legislation continued throughout the spring and into the summer.

Comparative Capsule 4.1 Domestic Policy Priorities

BIDEN	TRUMP
Address pandemic needs and help the economy to recover	Repeal Obamacare and stimulate economic growth
Buy American-made products	Defend the beliefs, cultures, and practices of his supporters
End racial discrimination	Keep communities safe, and punish criminal behavior
Reform immigration laws and procedures and increase the number of legal immigrants	Decrease the number of legal immigrants, Prevent illegal entry, and deport illegal residents
Climate change is real and must be addressed quickly	Climate change has been cyclical since the Earth formed

Other Priorities

During his first 100 days, Biden signed ten acts of Congress into law and issued 42 executive orders, more than half of them reversing Trump's actions. He also addressed other critical matters, most of which required legislation to change public policy. Although there was broad public support for improving transportation, communications, and environmental matters, other proposals evolved political and legal controversy. Foremost among them was voting rights.

Voting

Democrats proposed legislation that would automatically register eligible citizens, extend the period for early voting, facilitate the distribution and extend the deadlines for mail-in ballots, eliminate partisan gerrymandering, and publicize the names and contributions made to nonparty groups. *The Help America Vote Act of 2021* would have also made it difficult for states to prevent ex-felons from voting after they served their sentences.

President Biden strongly supported the legislation; the Republicans strongly opposed it, making Senate passage unlikely under rules that permitted a filibuster. Following the House's enactment of the legislation, Biden issued an executive order to federal agencies to aid the registration and voting for government workers, and Democratic state legislators introduced hundreds of proposals to expand voting rights, especially absentee voting.[21]

In addition, the *John R. Lewis Voting Rights Advancement Act of 2021*, named after the recently deceased civil rights leader and member of Congress, sought to reauthorize Justice Department reviews of voting laws in states that had a long history of discrimination. The Supreme Court had ended this review in the case of *Shelby v. Holder* in 2013.

The legislation was aimed at new state laws that Republican legislatures enacted after the 2020 elections to strengthen ID requirements, limit the automatic distribution of mail-in ballots, and shorten the time for early voting.[22] By the middle of May, 20 states had enacted such laws.

The Republicans claimed that the legislation was necessary to prevent fraudulent voting practices, which Trump said contributed to his 2020 defeat. Democrats, on the other hand, perceived the new state laws as adversely affecting minority voting and contended in legal challenges that they violated the Fourteenth Amendment's equal protection clause, but the Supreme Court had held in its *Brnovich v. the Democratic National Committee* decision in 2021 that restrictions placed in Arizona's voting law did not. Nonetheless, President Biden called these newly enacted state laws "un-American and sick, Jim Crow in the 21st Century."[23]

Partisan political action committees and private sector corporations within states that changed their voting laws also got involved. Major League Baseball actually moved its 2021 All-Star Game out of Atlanta because of the changes in Georgia's new voting rules. The controversy was all about future electoral success. Partisans of both parties saw voter participation as a key factor in the outcome of elections.

Policing

Other significant political issues were criminal justice and reforming police methods. House Democrats enacted the *George Floyd Justice in Policing Act of 2021*, which was designed to reduce the use of excessive force in arrests, enhance police accountability, and limit their immunity in misconduct lawsuits.

Biden, who had urged such reforms as a presidential candidate, said he would appoint a commission to study the problem if elected, but subsequently decided not to do so, although he continued to speak out on the matter and was sympathetic to the Black Lives Matter movement.

Unionization

Similarly, during Biden's first 100 days, the House passed a measure to protect the right of workers to organize, especially in right-to-work states. The timing of this bill coincided with efforts in Alabama to unionize an Amazon distribution facility. Biden backed this proposal but did not mention Amazon in his support of unionization. Employees of that company voted against joining the union by a margin of more than two to one. The president also issued an order to departments and agencies in the executive branch to identify policies that would discourage federal workers from organizing and forming unions.

Gun Control

After a series of mass killings in Georgia, Colorado, and California, the Biden administration addressed a perennial issue, gun control, by regulating the purchase of homemade firearms known as "ghost guns," which were used in shootings. Such guns have no serial numbers. Citing a Justice Department's report on gun violence, the president issued an executive order requiring background checks on people purchasing equipment to make or enlarge the capacity of their firearms. A poll taken by *Politico* indicated public support for this action.[24]

Democrats, including the president, were in favor of even more restrictive controls on firearms. They wanted to reenact a ban on assault weapons that had expired in 2004, institute universal background checks for gun purchasers, and require a designated waiting period before firearms could be obtained, but Republican and some Democratic lawmakers opposed any legislation that impinged on gun ownership. It took until the end of June 2022 for a compromise to be reached that strengthened and expanded background checks on young purchasers of firearms but did not address the assault weapons issue.

Budget

Biden introduced his first budget summary for the 2022 Fiscal Year in April, a little over two weeks after the deputy budget director had been confirmed. The nominee for director had withdrawn her nomination when it became clear that she would not be confirmed. No other person had been nominated, much less designated, for that position by the time Biden's budget outline was announced. It was not until May 28 that a more detailed budget that included funding for all the major proposals that the president had proposed was released.

All of these pending issues suggested that tough legislative going lay ahead for Biden and the closely divided Congress. During the first 100 days, Kamala Harris cast four tie-breaking votes in the Senate, and the president achieved only one major legislative victory, the *American Rescue Plan Act*. The polarized political climate in Congress showed no signs of abating.

Notes

1. Only 43 percent expressed a great deal or fair amount of trust and confidence in the executive branch of government in a poll conducted by the Gallup organization from August 31, 2020, to September 13, 2020. Only 33 percent expressed similar confidence in Congress during that same period. "Trends from A-Z: Trust in Government," *Gallup Poll*.
2. Lydia Saad, "U.S. Satisfaction Sinks With Many Aspects of Public Life," *Gallup Poll*, February 4, 2021.
3. David Cohen, "Majority Blame Trump for Jan. 6 Rioting; but Not Most Republicans," *Politico*, January 17, 2021.
4. Jeffrey M. Jones, "Support for Third U.S. Political Party at High Point," *Gallup Poll*, February 15, 2021. The poll was conducted after Biden took office but before the Senate's impeachment trial.
5. Kendall Karson, "Impeachment Trial Solidified Views on Trump's Conviction: POLL," *ABC News*, February 15, 2021.
6. Kelly Mema and Jason Hoffman, "Biden Says 'Democracy Must Always Be Defended' After Trump's Acquittal in Second Impeachment Trial," *CNN*, February 13, 2021.
7. Andrew Romaro, "Yahoo News/YouGov Poll: More Than Two-Thirds of Americans Side With Biden on COVID-19 Relief—And Most Support the Rest of His Agenda," *Yahoo News/Entertainment*, February 1, 2021. The poll was taken on Inauguration Day and the day after it.
8. Ashley Parker, Matt Viser, and Seung Min Kim, "On COVID Relief, Compromise May Not Be Biden's Priority," *Washington Post*, February 8, 2021.
9. Jasmine Mithani, Aaron Bycoffe, Christopher Groskopf, and Dhrumil Mehta, "How Americans View Biden's Response to the Coronavirus Crisis," *Fivethirtyeight.com*, February 16, 2021.

10. Cary Funk and Alec Tyson, "Growing Share of Americans Say They Plan to Get a COVID-19 Vaccine—Or Already Have," *Pew Research Center*, March 5, 2021.

11. Annie Karin and Zolan Kanno-Youngs, "As Biden Confronts Vaccine Hesitancy, Republicans Are a Particular Challenge," *New York Times*, March 15, 2021.

12. "COVID-19 Vaccinations in the United States," *Centers for Disease Control and Prevention*, accessed April 30, 2021.

13. "Topics From A–Z: Immigration," *Gallup Poll*.

14. The Centers for Disease Control and Prevention's (CDC) policy of delaying evictions and foreclosures during the pandemic was also subjected to legal challenge, although the CDC subsequently extended its policy from March 30 to June 30, 2021.

15. It takes more than two years for the courts to resolve asylum cases. By the end of March 2021, there were 1.3 million people seeking asylum in the United States.

16. Reade Levinson, Kristina Cooke, and Mica Rosenberg, "Special Report: How Trump Administration Left Indelible Mark on U.S. Immigration Courts," *Reuters*, March 8, 2021. In 2019, 71 percent of the cases involving unaccompanied minors resulted in deportation, a reason that many do not return for their scheduled court dates but reside in the country illegally. Maria Abi-Habib, "Young Migrants to U.S., Halted One Mile Short," *New York Times*, April 3, 2021.

17. Phillip Wegmann, "Real Clear Politics Poll," *Real Clear Politics*, March 30, 2021.

18. Will Weissert and Hannah Fingerhut, "AP-NORC Poll: Border Woes Dent Biden's Approval on Immigration," *Associated Press*, April 5, 2021.

19. Julie Watson, "Refugee Admissions Hit Record Low, Despite Biden's Reversal," *Associated Press*, October 5, 2021.

20. Mike Zapler, Eli Okon, and Garrett Ross, "Playbook PM," *Politico*, April 14, 2021.

21. "Voting Laws Roundup: March 2021," *Brennen Center for Justice*, April 1, 2021.

22. Ibid.

23. Peter W. Stevenson, "Expand Access? A Historic Restriction? What the Georgia Voting Law Really Does," *Washington Post*, April 5, 2021.

24. Ryan Lizza, Rachael Bode, Eugene Daniels, and Tara Palmeri, "Politico Playbook," *Politico*, April 14, 2021.

CHAPTER 5
RESTRUCTURING FOREIGN POLICY

Biden had criticized Trump for withdrawing the United States from the Paris Climate Accords, the World Health Organization, and the multinational agreement with Iran to restrict the development of its nuclear program. When he took office, he announced that the United States would rejoin these groups, but Iran refused to participate in further talks if the United States was involved. Biden also approved a five-year extension of the New START nuclear arms treaty with Russia.

Biden articulated the basic tenets of his foreign policy goals well before his presidency: defending America's vital interests, ending forever wars, elevating the use of diplomacy, restoring partnerships with traditional allies, promoting arms control and nuclear nonproliferation, and working with others to combat the harmful effects of climate change.

Perceiving that democracy versus authoritarianism would be the overriding issue for the next generation, he stated at his first news conference, "This is a battle between the utility of democracies in the 21st century and autocracies. We've got to prove democracy works."[1] He denounced violations of human rights by dictatorial regimes, even reaching back in history to refer to the mass killing of Armenians by the Ottoman Empire as a genocide.

Creating a Vibrant Policymaking and Implementation Process

The president wanted to share America's international leadership with major allies. He did not want to pursue the "America First" policy and personal diplomacy of the Trump presidency. Biden had criticized his predecessor's trade war with China; his failure to confront Russian hacking, election interference, and its hostilities against Ukraine; and Trump's personal relations with many of the world's most autocratic leaders.

DOI: 10.4324/9781003176978-7

To replace the previous administration's priorities on the country's economic interests, religious freedoms, and property rights, the president proposed what he termed "a foreign policy for the middle class," one in which the benefits of a skilled, productive, and well-compensated labor force, innovation by entrepreneurs, and technological advances in manufacturing would enhance America's stature and competitiveness in the international community. In his inaugural address, he said, "We will lead not merely by the example of our power, by the power of our example. We'll be a strong and trusted partner for peace, progress, and security."[2]

Developing a Biden doctrine for foreign affairs took time. Although the administration reacted more quickly to military actions that adversely affected national security (such as the attacks on American troops and their allies in Syria, the Russian buildup of troops and offensive weapons near the Ukrainian border, China's growing military presence and threatening actions in Asia, as well as the Taliban's in Afghanistan), newer policy adjustments were slower to be designed and implemented.[3]

The first step in framing a policy in foreign affairs was to set his administration's geographic priorities: the Pacific, Western Europe, and the Western Hemisphere, but not the Middle East.[4] The second was to conduct strategic reviews of relations, alliances, and threats by the appropriate diplomatic, military, and intelligence officials, especially the White House's national security staff.

In choosing his foreign policy team, Biden selected experienced diplomats and policy experts, many of whom served in the civil service or as political appointees in previous Democratic administrations, think tanks, and his transition staff. Most were internationalists who saw diplomatic engagement as the principal vehicle for strengthening alliances, fostering cooperation, and opposing actions that threatened democratic nations in general and the United States in particular.

Biden enlarged and restructured his National Security Council (NSC) staff to deal with the new priorities he established and the current issues that had to be addressed: cybersecurity, adverse climate change, and the worldwide COVID-19 pandemic. He revitalized morale and filled vacancies in the State and Defense Departments, and he removed most Trump appointees from these and the intelligence agencies. The *Washington Post* reported that by the end of 2020, half of the top 60 positions in the Department of Defense were not held by a Senate-confirmed nominee but by Trump's political appointees,[5] but the Trump administration had also purposely and profoundly diminished the role and influence of senior civil servants in the State and Defense Departments and many of the intelligence agencies, prompting experienced and knowledgeable career officials, especially in the Department of State, to leave government service. Consequently, the first two departments President Biden visited were State and Defense to demonstrate his understanding of the difficulties they faced with the previous administration. Biden also enlarged and refocused the NSC staff.

The slowness of the confirmation process contributed to the Biden administration's start-up problems and forced it to designate acting deputies to facilitate planning and decision-making in the early months. Biden was also slow in sending the nominations of ambassadors to the Senate, much to the dismay of foreign governments and major Democratic donors who sought plush ambassadorial appointments. Biden tended to select people experienced in foreign affairs, particularly career foreign service officers for smaller countries in Asia and Central and South America.

A majority of Americans (60 percent) expressed confidence in Biden's ability to make sound foreign policy decisions, with Democrats expressing more confidence (88 percent) than Republicans (27 percent). A large majority also supported the president's shared global approach in contrast to Trump's go-it-alone policy.[6]

Photo 5.1 *Lloyd Austin Sworn in as Secretary of Defense*
Source: *AP Photo/Evan Vucci*

Ongoing Diplomacy With Allies and Adversaries

Conversations with America's neighbors and Western European leaders were first held to reaffirm the president's intention to maintain friendly relations and address common concerns. A principal issue with Canada was Biden's decision to terminate the Keystone Pipeline. Naturally, Canadian leaders were unhappy, although they supported reducing harmful effects on the environment.

Mexico, overburdened with the masses of immigrants from Central America traveling to the United States, agreed to close its southern border for a month; the United States sent 2.5 million doses of the coronavirus vaccines to Mexico and 1.5 million to Canada, although the Biden administration denied it was a quid-pro-quo deal. Russia and China had been giving their vaccines to poorer countries to improve their relations and influence with the underdeveloped world. Biden pledged to do the same.

The Asian dimension of American policy was also addressed by visits of the Secretaries of State and Defense to South Korea, where they reiterated that the United States would protect that country from an attack from the North with military resources. They also expressed support for a denuclearized Korean Peninsula. Joint military exercises continued to be conducted; North Korea responded with verbal threats and two missiles fired into the sea.

To reinforce American alliances and counter Chinese influence, Secretary of State Tony Blinken organized virtual monthly meetings with Australia, India, and Japan (the Quad) to coordinate economic competition with China and oppose its territorial expansion. The United States offered to help India cope with a massive COVID-19 outbreak by extending technological and financial aid to produce the vaccines it needed.

Biden perceived China to be America's major adversary in Asia; he favored a policy of economic and technological competition, not military confrontation, but also repeated his resolve to defend Taiwan's security, criticized the crackdown on democratic opposition in Hong Kong, and criticized its treatment of Uyghur Muslims. A formal but contentious meeting between Chinese and U.S. foreign policy leaders in Alaska in mid-March produced no new breakthroughs.

Initially, there was less focus on Russian authoritarianism, although in an interview, Biden had said that he agreed with the perception that

Russian President Vladimir Putin was a "killer," a remark that the Russian government vigorously denounced, even to the point of recalling its U.S. ambassador. Nonetheless, Putin agreed to participate in a summit that Biden called to discuss climate change.

For the other major actions in which Biden had accused Russia, cyber hacking and election meddling, the president imposed sanctions, preventing American financial institutions from purchasing bonds or lending money to Russia's Central Bank and its National Wealth Fund. He also imposed penalties on the Russian individuals and companies involved, expelling ten diplomats in the United States who were presumably engaged in intelligence activities; Russia responded in a similar fashion by banning ten American diplomats.

As the United States reevaluated its involvement in the Middle East, the planned pull out of American forces in Afghanistan by the Trump administration in May was delayed but not terminated on the advice of military, intelligence, and foreign policy officials who feared their withdrawal would result in more territorial gains by the Taliban and the possible collapse of the Afghanistan government. Biden was determined, however, to end America's involvement in "forever wars," saying, "I am now the fourth United States president to preside over an American troop presence in Afghanistan. Two Republicans. Two Democrats. I will not pass this responsibility to a fifth."[7]

The United States also tried to diminish its role in the war-torn Middle East. Voicing support for Israel, acknowledging Jerusalem as its capital, and renewing aid to the Palestinian authority, the administration did not sponsor another negotiated peace effort but tried to achieve stability in the region by fostering an alliance with Egypt, Jordan, and the United Arab Emirates, three countries that conducted diplomatic relations with Israel.

The American people evidenced little concern about foreign policy issues other than immigration during the first 100 days of the Biden administration. Polls did not reveal many changes in Americans' attitudes toward other countries, friend or foe. China, Russia, North Korea, Iran, Iraq, and Libya were viewed most unfavorably by three-quarters of the American public, while traditional allies in West Europe and East Asia were perceived most favorably.[8] Other than immigration, there was little sustained criticism of Biden's foreign policy, including the president's determination to withdraw the remaining American troops from Afghanistan, which is discussed in Chapter 13.

Comparative Capsule 5.1   Foreign Policy Priorities

BIDEN	TRUMP
Promote internationalism	Promote "America First"
Reorient geographic priorities	
Foster cooperative leadership	Emphasize presidential-led diplomacy
Rejoin and strengthen popular world agreements; participate in multinational negotiations	Withdraw from Paris Climate Accord and World Health Organization
Strengthen NATO	Get NATO countries to pay their fair share
Design a doctrine based on realism	Design a doctrine based on power
Improve relationships among allies and stand up to foes of the United States	Criticize China and its communist leadership and trust Russia and President Putin

The Climate Initiative

To demonstrate continuing concern with climate change, redeem his pledge to rejoin the international agreements, and contribute to efforts to improve the environment, Biden invited the leaders of 40 countries and other experts and dignitaries, including the Pope, to a virtual climate summit in April 2021. Noting the time was short to reverse the adverse effects of fossil fuel emissions and forest destruction, the president urged the international community to extend its climate control efforts and pledged that the United States would cut its own emissions in half by 2030. Other foreign leaders made similar pledges to decrease dependence on fossil fuels, cut gas emissions, and provide financial assistance to less-developed countries to strengthen their economies without damaging the environment.

New energy technologies were costly, potentially economically disruptive, and socially transformative, but Biden argued that the benefits outweighed the costs and would create thousands of new jobs. The debate and actions on climate change would remain a domestic and international issue throughout and beyond Biden's term of office.

A majority of Americans continue to believe that climate change is a major problem and that the government should regulate greenhouse gases, although the partisan gap has widened with Democrats overwhelmingly supportive of government regulations to do so but a majority of Republicans not supportive.[9]

Notes

1. David E. Sanger, "Biden Defines His Underlying Challenge with China: 'Prove Democracy Works,'" *New York Times*, March 26, 2021.
2. President Joe Biden's Inaugural Address, January 20, 2021, *White House.*
3. Biden imposed sanctions on Russia for the poisoning and imprisonment of Alexei Navalny; released a previously classified intelligence report on the killing of journalist Jamal Khashoggi by Saudi Arabian authorities, although the report did not mention the Crown Prince's involvement; and delayed U.S. troop withdrawal in Afghanistan.
4. The president did say that he would keep the U.S. embassy in Jerusalem and supported a two-state solution to the Arab–Israeli conflict.
5. Dan Diamond, Lisa Rein, and Julliet Ellperin, "After Trump, Biden Is Working to Rebuild the Government," *Washington Post*, February 6, 2021.
6. "Majority of Americans Confident in Biden's Handling of Foreign Policy as Term Begins," *Pew Research Center*, February 24, 2021.
7. Aamer Madhani and Matthew Lee, "Biden to Pull U.S. Troops from Afghanistan to End 'Forever War,'" *Associated Press*, April 14, 2021.
8. "Topics A–Z: Country Ratings," *Gallup Poll.*
9. Darrell Fears and Emily Guskin, "Poll: Recent Climate Disasters Haven't Swayed Opinions of Many Americans," *Washington Post*, November 13, 2021.

PART III

PRESIDENTIAL–INSTITUTIONAL RELATIONSHIPS

CHAPTER 6
THE BIDEN ADMINISTRATION'S LEGISLATIVE STYLE

Separate Institutions Sharing Powers

"An invitation to struggle" is how Professor Edward S. Corwin described the constitutional relationship between Congress and the presidency.[1] Presidents try to set the legislative agenda, influence the enactment of their policy priorities, and use the veto or threaten it, if their programmatic desires are not met. Theodore Roosevelt proposed the first comprehensive program to Congress; Woodrow Wilson, the second. Then beginning with Franklin Roosevelt's first 100 days, legislative programming became an important expectation of modern presidents with the election campaign shaping their initial policy agenda.

The presidency's constitutional responsibilities, however, did not increase with the institution's expanded legislative role, although some of its statutory powers did. For most presidents, their legislative influence depended on external factors, such as the partisan composition of Congress, the severity of crises that had to be addressed, the size of their electoral victory, and their own leadership skills.[2] Franklin Roosevelt, Lyndon Johnson, Barack Obama, and, to a limited extent, Ronald Reagan had these political advantages in the era of modern presidents; others did not.

Partisan divisions in Congress and the intensity of those divisions have added to or impeded presidential success. The deep and wide political polarization of the country and especially within the Congress; the opposing ideological orientations of Democrats and Republicans; the deterioration of personal relationships among members of both legislative bodies; and the larger-than-normal egos of elected officials have magnified the problems of finding common ground to resolve the

DOI: 10.4324/9781003176978-9

nation's problems, especially when government is divided, which it has been most of the time since 1968.

There are also institutional rivalries that affect the president's exercise of power. In the making of foreign policy, especially the exercise of war powers, the president's influence and policymaking have increased and role of Congress in this policy area has declined. In 1973, the *War Powers Resolution* sought to give Congress more authority when presidents order the military into battle. A written report to Congress within 48 hours and congressional approval within 60 to 90 days is required by the legislation or U.S. forces have to be withdrawn. These constraints have not stopped or even reduced contemporary presidents from using force in situations deemed to threaten U.S. national interests and security. During the 117th Congress, a group of liberal Democrats and libertarian Republicans tried to increase Congress's role in foreign policy by proposing to give the legislature the power to reverse arms sales and executive agreements that the president had approved. The Biden White House has vigorously opposed this proposal.

Within the domestic arena, former President Trump initiated legal action in October 2021 to prevent senior officials who served in his administration from testifying before a congressional committee investigating the January 6 Capitol riot. Trump's lawyers argued that oral conversations and written correspondence to and from the president were protected by executive privilege, but Biden rejected that claim. He believed that the public had a right to know about the previous administration's involvement in the riot and that the committee's subpoenas were justified. Most of Trump's advocates refused to testify or refused to answer, pleading the Fifth Amendment right not to incriminate oneself.

The news media emphasize and magnify the conflicts within and between president and Congress. They also focus on the policymaking process, the personalities involved, and the positions they take that make or break the deal. The proliferation and polarization of news sources since the 1980s, magnified by a confirmation bias of their audiences, have contributed to a decline of trust in elected officials and a reduction of confidence in government that has extended over five decades. Achieving major policy change under these conditions has been extremely difficult for presidents of both parties.

Unified government is a slightly different story if the majority party is sufficiently large and unified. It was on many but not all issues during the administrations of Franklin Roosevelt, Lyndon Johnson, most of George W. Bush's term in office, and the first two years of the Clinton, Obama, and Trump presidencies. Moving quickly highlights a president's leadership credentials, which, in turn, maximizes public support and improves the prospects that the president's policy proposals will be enacted into law.

Biden's Legislative Dilemma

When Biden assumed the presidency, he encountered more favorable than unfavorable political conditions. He had a small majority in the House and an evenly divided Senate in which the vice president could cast a tie-breaking vote. Although the country was divided along partisan lines, there was a consensus on the most important issue that needed to be addressed first: the pandemic and its adverse impact on the economy. To do so successfully, Biden had to contend with ideological divisions within and between the major parties and also a populace that had lost confidence in government and in its leadership.

Mired between the desire to act quickly to combat and control the pandemic and to try to bring the country together by reaching out to a variety of contending and competing voices, he chose to do both, but at different times and by different legislative processes. He opted to prioritize the pandemic and its economic impact, which Americans overwhelmingly believed to be the most urgent problem, by letting his party's leadership in the House of Representatives design and draft *The American Rescue Plan Act of 2021*. Since Democrats in the Senate lacked sufficient votes to overcome a filibuster, they had to use the reconciliation process to enact the legislation, alienating Republicans and undermining Biden's bipartisan approach. Republicans had taken the same route in 2017 for their tax reduction bill.

The President's Way of Exercising Congressional Leadership

Biden's style in dealing with Congress was different from his predecessors. Unlike Trump and Obama, he invited members of Congress to the White House. During his first 100 days, more than 100 members of both parties attended discussions of public policy in the White House with the president and his senior aides. Biden seemed to enjoy these sessions and the give-and-take that occurred in them. It helped him to build and rebuild personal relationships, which he thought was a key factor in getting legislation enacted into law. It also was the way he worked with Congress as a senator and as Obama's vice president.

At these meetings, the president engaged participants, listened to their arguments, and even shared personal stories to lighten the political climate. According to many of the invitees of both parties, he was personable, friendly, and authentic, attributes that his three immediate predecessors lacked.[3] Chocolate chip cookies, Biden's favorite, were wrapped in a presidential seal and given as departing gifts.

The president usually did not make policy decisions during these sessions. Decision-making in his White House was a collaborative process, involving senior advisors, policy experts, and party leaders, mostly Democratic. The president's conversations with Republican leaders were conducted privately and mostly by phone.

Personal relations are Biden's leadership strength. Although disagreements were articulated in public by both sides and highlighted by the news media, the president avoided much of the personal accusations that plagued and stereotyped his predecessors. He was viewed as a nice guy.

Photo 6.1 *President Biden, in the company of a bipartisan group of Senators, speaks to the press outside the White House in June 2021*
Source: AP Photo/Jacquelyn Martin

Lobbying From Within

The White House's ongoing relations with Congress are conducted primarily by its Legislative Affairs Office. That office was created during the Eisenhower administration. Today it is housed in the East Wing of the White House, the wing that is closest to Capitol Hill. Tunnels under the Treasury Department allow members of Congress and their staffs to enter the White House without incurring contact with news media representatives.

Most of the principal liaison staff of the president operate on Capitol Hill, using mobile phones and as bases, the offices of their party's whips. Their major function is to communicate with members and their staffs and report information they consider critical to the White House. They also count votes, twist arms, and provide services to members of Congress and their constituents.

With the exception of congressional party leaders, phone calls and visits to the president and vice president from members of Congress have to go through the Legislative Affairs Office, which evaluates the purpose of the communication, briefs the White House, and if approved by the chief of staff, schedules the appointment. In the first four months of the Biden administration, the staff arranged for more than 150 visits from members of Congress.

Biden's legislative staff consists of about 15 aides who work "the Hill" and an equal number of White House–based support personnel. Louisa Terrell, who worked for Biden in the Senate and for Obama in his legislative affairs office, headed the president's congressional lobbying activities. Her deputies and their aides also have considerable congressional experience.

Knowing members of Congress and their staff is critical to access, to credibility, to servicing the president's needs, and to exerting influence. Successful lobbying is built on personal relationships that may take years to establish. Contacts with congressional personnel are made by phone, Zoom, and after the pandemic, meetings in congressional offices, food venues, and social events.

To be successful, lobbyists need to be informed about ongoing White House discussions and decisions. When they are not, confusion, consternation, and criticism can result. Biden's meetings with Republican negotiators on the infrastructure bill is a case in point. The legislative staff was not fully informed of the president's willingness to compromise on certain issues; they continued to assert as the administration's initial position. Republicans complained that the White House was backing off the president's bipartisan approach, a position that almost undermined the negotiations.[4]

Mobilizing Public Support

The White House has orchestrated numerous public campaigns to heighten its lobbying efforts in Congress, promote its legislative accomplishments, and counter GOP criticism. The communications and outreach offices cite polling data regularly to illustrate favorable public opinion on most of the president's top priorities. Both social media and traditional communications strategies are used to reach sympathetic audiences.

In its public relations strategy to increase the number of people getting vaccinated, the White House reached out to the medical community, not celebrities as had been originally planned, as well as to groups that had lower rates of vaccinations. They even encouraged data apps to indicate vaccination status of individuals seeking to meet others and locations for them to obtain shots. When the Delta variant surged in the summer and the president directed mask wearing in federal facilities, the White House officials accused the news media of heightening the problem, much like Trump protested the press's "COVID, COVID, COVID" headlined stories. An anonymous White House official was quoted as saying, "The media's coverage doesn't match the moment. . . . It has been hyperbolic and frankly irresponsible in a way that hardens vaccine hesitancy."[5]

As part of its general public relations campaign on infrastructure legislation, the White House encouraged Democratically oriented PACs and interest groups to educate and energize their clientele on the new jobs, better and safer ground transportation, and improved public transit issues that would result from the legislation. They sent fact sheets and other information to local news media and opened the press secretary's regular briefings to reporters to virtual participation from smaller media outlets; government aides and policy experts were made available for interviews; and projects that affected specific geographic areas were emphasized.

Republican PACs, outside interest groups, and private companies also increased their substantive policy advertising in the spring of 2021.

Spending on Facebook and other social and traditional media increased. Much of the GOP counter to the administration's public vaccination initiative focused on criticism of Dr. Anthony Fauci, the head of the government infectious disease office, after a large number of his emails became public.[6] Infrastructure objections focused on the costs and hinted that they would result in higher taxes on paychecks.

Negotiating: The White House, Congress, and the Public

The president's strategy on the *Build Back Better Act* was different. It was more private than public, with more one-on-one meetings and conversations with members of Congress after bill signing events or on trips in which members were present. After Congress returned from its Labor Day recess, Biden held few public events but participated in meetings with groups of Democratic members of Congress. Their small House majority and evenly divided Senate required almost complete partisan unity, and Biden sought to achieve it. Negotiating behind the scenes and quieting the bully pulpit with less concern about public opinion and more about Democratic opinion, the White House focused its activities on Congress. In trying to find common ground among Democrats, the president used the connection between legislative achievements and the party's short- and long-term electoral success as his principal motivating factor for compromise between moderates and progressives.[7] And he was successful. His leadership stature rose as a consequence.

Comparative Capsule 6.1 Relations with Members of Congress	
BIDEN	**TRUMP**
Invited members of Congress of both parties to the White House	Invited fewer and only Republican members to the White House
Tried to establish personal friendships and relationships with most Democrats, some Republicans in Congress	Ridiculed both Democrats and Republicans who spoke or voted against his policy positions
Deferred initially to Democratic leadership and chairs to draft legislation and negotiated with them when he had problems with their drafts	Involved fewer Republican members of Congress and dealt primarily with the leadership and a few others, in detailing and negotiating his priorities into legislation
Helped to unify Democratic voting in Congress on most partisan issues	Was unable to control Republicans in Congress on some partisan issues

Notes

1. Edward S. Corwin, *The President: Office and Powers* (New York: New York University Press, 1984).
2. Richard E. Neustadt, *Presidential Power* (New York: Wiley, 1960).
3. Lisa Mascaro, "Chocolate Chip Diplomacy: Biden Courts Congress with Gusto," *Associated Press*, April 23, 2021.
4. Alexandra Jaffe and Josh Boak, "WH Legislative Team Pursues 'Politics Is Personal' Strategy," *Associated Press*, May 29, 2021.
5. Oliver Darcy, "White House Vents Frustration With 'Hyperbolic Delta Coverage,'" *CNN Business*, August 2, 2021.
6. "Companies Put Their Advertising Dollars Behind Public Affairs Issues," *Bully Pulpit Interactive*, June 10, 2021.
7. Christopher Cadelago and Marianne Levine, "Biden Bets His Agenda on the Inside Game," *Politico*, October 19, 2021.

CHAPTER 7
LEGISLATIVE ACHIEVEMENTS, DELAYS, AND FAILURES

After his initial success in gaining the enactment of the *American Rescue Plan Act of 2021* and the confirmation of his cabinet-level nominees, Biden's legislative challenges and difficulties became more arduous, time consuming, and difficult. They also became increasingly relevant for his future legislative relations, the midterm elections, and the president's stature as a legislative leader.

Parameters of the President's Legislative Powers and Constraints

Chapter 6 noted constraints on and sources of the president's legislative influence. Constraints included the constitutional structure, the Senate's filibuster rules, the small numerical advantage the Democrats had in the House and the evenly divided Senate, the deep-seated partisan polarization that unified the opposition, and personal and internal institutional rivalries. The strengths included partisan control of both chambers of Congress, an electoral victory, unsatisfactory conditions that needed to be improved, and the president's nonabrasive style and personal manner. Public opinion varied with conditions and perceived successes and failures but did so along clear partisan lines. The partisan divisions themselves and the country remained fairly stable at rough partisan parity, with the percentage of self-identified Independents increasing.

Senate rules sparked controversy from the outset and were considered a major issue during the last several administrations. The minority gained leverage from the filibuster rule and vehemently opposed changing it. The majority did not. In fact, Democrats became so frustrated by the minority opposing judicial nominations of President Obama that Senate Majority Leader Harry Reid introduced the "nuclear option" in 2013 to

DOI: 10.4324/9781003176978-10

prevent killing nominations by filibustering them. After Donald Trump, the Republican-controlled Senate did the same, reaffirming the rule in 2017, to confirm Neil Gorsuch as a Supreme Court Justice.

Holding up nominees impeded governing but did not prevent it. Filibustering appropriations to run the government did. In 1974, Congress enacted a law that permitted the legislature to reconcile financial differences by a simple majority vote. First used in 1980, the reconciliation process has continued to be a way of circumventing the Senate rule for unlimited debate on budgetary matters.

Progressive Democrats wanted to eliminate the filibuster rule entirely in 2021, aware of how filibustering had been used in the past to stop legislation on civil rights. Republicans wanted to keep the rule to give them some leverage to influence policymaking or prevent policy they opposed from becoming law. Some Democrats objected to abolishing the rule as well, believing that they would need it someday if they were in the minority and that partisan turnover in elections would result in radical policy change. President Biden did not favor eliminating the rule, although he did become more open to modifying it as it threatened to derail his major policy proposals. Thus, the choice came down to bipartisan compromises or reconciliation in which a plurality would prevail. What constituted budgetary matters became another issue, one that the Senate Parliamentarian initially decided.

Major Legislative Accomplishments

The American Rescue Plan Act of 2021

The president decided to take the reconciliation route for his stimulus legislation. He did so for several reasons. Given the state of the economy and the pandemic, he believed that time was of the essence. He pursued a reconciliation strategy with *The American Rescue Plan Act of 2021* because he did not want to engage in lengthy negotiations that delayed action, watered down his proposal, or magnified criticism from Republicans and progressive Democrats. The president's success in doing so was a consequence of converging factors: the magnitude of the crisis, general public support for the stimulus and unemployment extension, and unity within the Democratic Party's congressional coalition.

The act provided for stimulus payments of $1,400 to individuals earning $75,000 or less and couples earning $150,000 or less, extended unemployment eligibility and payments, provided federal assistance for mortgage and rental payments based on income levels, and expanded childcare assistance and tax credits through the end of the year. It also increased the government's supplemental nutrition program, provided funding for increased COVID testing and vaccine distributions, and provided emergency grants to state and local governments, loans to small businesses, and emergency aid to elementary and secondary schools. The cost of the legislation was estimated to be $1.9 trillion, one of the most expensive economic emergency plans in American history.

Infrastructure Investment and Jobs Act (2021)

The next legislative item on Biden's agenda was the restoration of the nation's infrastructure. The convergence of forces that helped the president and fellow Democrats enact the *American Rescue Plan Act* was not nearly as cohesive for the infrastructure program that included climate change, greater economic and social equity, and a host of other issues.

Biden chose the bipartisan route for the infrastructure bill. He did so for several reasons. Some Republicans had indicated support for restoring the infrastructure during the Trump administration, although a bill was never enacted into law. After using reconciliation for the *American Rescue Plan Act*, Biden wanted to demonstrate to the GOP that he still favored bipartisan legislation; he believed that it would help him on future issues on which his party was not nearly as unified and that elected officials could and should work together to promote national interests. He yearned for the days of the old Senate, which he remembered as less hostile and a more productive legislative environment in which he had felt comfortable, and believed many of his longtime colleagues desired that as well rather than just a podium to appeal to their electoral supporters.

In mid-May, Biden met with the bipartisan leadership of Congress, the first time he had done so since he assumed the presidency, although he had been in touch with them by phone. He then invited to the Oval Office a group of Republican senators who had indicated that they were open to compromise on the legislation. They countered Biden's more comprehensive $2.5 trillion proposal, which included spending on climate improvement and social welfare, with a plan to spend $586 billion on the physical components of the infrastructure. Although the president offered to reduce the amount of the original package by $550 billion, the two sides were still far apart. Biden continued to talk with Senator Shelley Moore Capito (WV), a leader of the Republican negotiating team, but to no avail. When their discussions ended without agreement, the president turned to another group of ten Republicans and ten moderate Democrats to see if some compromise could be reached. Box 7.1 describes the history of infrastructure legislation, the 2021 negotiations on the bill between Democrats and Republicans, and also the Senate and House, and the individual participants and their policy positions. It was a battle royal among Democrats.

Box 7.1 The Bipartisan Infrastructure Bill: Pros and Cons

History

Before the country existed, Native Americans and settlers built roads, ports, and waterways for travel and trade. The second Continental Congress established the U.S. postal system in 1775 to facilitate the exchange of written correspondence, public debate, and newsworthy events. In the 1840s, a telegraph system began to be developed with the help of Congress and was consolidated into a national communication network. Local railroads were built, roads paved, and bridges and tunnels constructed as critical connective structures. The first transcontinental railroad line was completed in 1869. The development of electricity and the connection of local electric grids into a national system began in the 1870s and was completed over the next 50 years. It spurred the development and speed of communications (telegraph, telephone, radio, television, eventually computer connections) and travel (railroads, automobiles, and airplanes). It was powered primarily by water and fossil fuels.

Much of the construction was funded by local and state governments and private entrepreneurs. During the Great Depression, Franklin Roosevelt created the Works Progress Administration and vastly expanded road building, which the popularity of the automobile demanded. The Tennessee Valley Authority expanded the electric grid in rural areas in the South. In the mid-20th century, the Eisenhower administration began the construction of an interstate highway system and new and larger airports.

The expansion of the population, the increasing modes of communication and transportation, and public use of them put strains on the system and its structural underpinnings. Maintenance has not kept up with usage. Increasingly, the country's infrastructure has become a national problem in need of fixing. Comprehensive legislation for doing so has not been enacted into law.

To improve the chances for passage in 2021, the Democrats created additional incentives for members of Congress to support the legislation. Earmarks, which allowed the designation of specific projects in specific congressional districts, were restored; the White House became more receptive to requests for projects, such as the need to repair the Brent Spence Bridge between Ohio and Kentucky, to rebuild and expand a railroad tunnel between New Jersey and New York City, and other proposals from around the country.

Biden's Plan

The president proposed legislation at the end of March. His plan was to rebuild 20,000 miles of roads, repair ten of the most economically important and least sound bridges, eliminate lead pipes that carry water, manufacture more electric cars and the accessories necessary to power them, improve and electrify public transportation, end environmental discrimination, improve and secure the nation's power grid, and expand broadband networks to all parts of the country. He said the programs would create thousands of new jobs and improve the environment. The original proposal would also extend social services to the needy.

Issues

Three fundamental issues divided partisans in consideration of the legislation. The first and most basic was the definition of infrastructure. The Republicans contended that it included the physical infrastructure: roads, bridges, tunnels, ship ports, and airports. They were also amendable to considering the electric grid and extending broadband networks as critical components. The Democrats' definition was much broader; in addition to the physical dimension, Democrats argued that there is also a human dimension that includes climate change, social services, and educational reforms.

The package the president proposed included both at a cost of $2.5 trillion. The plan with which the Republicans countered pertained only to physical structure and cost only about one-fourth of that amount. Most of the expenditures from the Republican plan were to come from existing appropriations, while most of the Democrats' plan consisted of new spending.

The third major difference was the source of revenue. Biden wanted to increase taxes on corporations and wealthy Americans; Republicans opposed any new taxes, not wanting to undermine the tax reductions they enacted in 2017. Instead, they proposed adjusting the gas tax to inflation, collecting fees from users, and using leftover funds from the *American Rescue Plan Act*. Biden, however, was opposed to taxing people with low incomes, which he believed user fees and increased gas taxes would do. Biden also suggested adding new inspectors to the Internal Revenue Service to catch and retain revenue from wealthy tax dodgers, which the Republicans also opposed, claiming that it was a new tax in disguise.

White House–Senate Negotiations

The first attempt at reaching common ground failed. After announcing his plan, the president and White House officials met with a group of ten Republicans led by Senator Shelley Moore Capito (WV). The Republicans indicated that they could support a narrower and less comprehensive proposal because they opposed additional spending for infrastructure projects. Their meeting with the president, although cordial, did not close the wide expenditure gap that divided both sides. Although Biden continued to talk with Capito, and some adjustments were proposed by each of them, the negotiators remained far apart. The differences were too great.

The president then turned to other moderate Republicans, such as Bill Cassidy (LA) and Rob Portman (OH), persuading them to join a new bipartisan negotiating group consisting of five senators from each party. The White House remained heavily involved in these negotiations with Biden's head of congressional liaison, Louisa Terrell, the director of the president's economic group, Brian Deese, and senior presidential advisor, Steve Ricchetti, representing the administration. They briefed the president several times a day on the progress of the negotiations. Lines of communication remained open between members of Congress and the White House. The president's legislative aides worked the phones and attended meetings on Capitol Hill.

After considerable discussion and haggling, both sides agreed on a framework for the bill that the president announced on June 24, 2021. The details of the framework still had to be worked out by the group, their staffs, and the White House negotiators.

The House Intercedes

Even before the actual bill was completed, opposition to it emerged in both legislative bodies. Speaker Nancy Pelosi said that the House of Representatives would not vote on the legislation until it enacted a massive reconciliation bill that progressive House Democrats wanted; Republicans, including those on the bipartisan committee, indicated that they would not be held hostage to the House, would not vote to limit debate until the actual legislation was introduced, and would not approve new taxes. Trump also announced that he opposed the bipartisan bill, even though he had supported one as president.

Pelosi's warning was prompted by progressive Democrats who feared that if the bipartisan bill was enacted, it might dilute the scope and size of the reconciliation bill that included climate improvement, educational reform, health care, and other social welfare programs. Attempting to placate angry progressive Democrats, Biden then said that he would refuse to sign the infrastructure bill "if it was sent to me without my Families Plan and other priorities, including clean energy."[1]

The president's remarks angered the Republican members of the committee who had agreed to the framework of the legislation. They voiced their concerns on various news shows, threatening to withhold their support for the bipartisan infrastructure bill if it was held hostage by the House. The president, caught in the middle, quickly clarified his remarks. In private calls to the Republicans on the committee and in a public statement, Biden said the two proposals were not linked, that he had given his word to the bipartisan group and would abide by it:

> At a press conference after announcing the bipartisan agreement, I indicated that I would refuse to sign the infrastructure bill if it was sent to me without my Families Plan and other priorities, including clean energy. . . . My comments also created the impression that I was issuing a veto threat on the very plan I had just agreed to, which was certainly not my intent.

> The bottom line is this: I gave my word to support the Infrastructure Plan, and that's what I intend to do. I intend to pursue the passage of that plan, which Democrats and Republicans agreed to on Thursday, with vigor. . . . I fully stand behind it without reservation or hesitation.[2]

The White House subsequently increased its behind-the-scenes efforts to save the compromise. Steve Ricchetti, one of the president's senior advisors, worked closely and continuously with the bipartisan group's two principal negotiators, Republican Rob Portman and Democrat Kyrsten Sinema. Meanwhile, other White House aides, including Chief of Staff Ron Klain, tried to placate progressive Democrats and others who had been excluded from the negotiations, especially Peter DeFazio, chair of the Transportation and Infrastructure COMMITTEE in the House. On July 28, the president announced that a deal had been finalized. But had it?

The Senate still had to vote on nonbinding amendments to the bill, which was to take all night. After defeating most of the amendments that could undercut parts of the legislation (known as poison pills), the Senate enacted the bipartisan infrastructure bill on August 10 by a 69 to 30 vote. It provided for $553 billion in new spending and extended for five years existing infrastructure spending that Congress had previously approved. The Congressional Budget Office estimated that the bill would add $256 billion over a ten-year period to the budget deficit. A majority of Americans favored the legislation.[3]

The bill was more than 2,700 pages long. Most of the provisions, which the administration and congressional supporters promoted, focused on transportation improvements: repairing and renovating roads, bridges, tunnels, ports, waterways, and airports and electrifying automobiles, trucks, and buses, along with building a national network of electric chargers. Sending the Senate-passed bill to the House was the next step. It was not expected to be a quick one. And it was not. The House had gone into summer recess, and its reconciliation bill had not been drafted. Prior to recessing, the Senate approved a 92-page set of budget instructions for the reconciliation bill on a straight party-line vote.

Despite public support for the bipartisan infrastructure bill, differences among House Democrats with progressives favoring Speaker Pelosi's plan to tie the infrastructure vote to the reconciliation vote on the *Build Back*

Better Act and a smaller group of moderates opposing it, stalled a House vote on the measure for almost three months. New deadlines were set but not met. When the Highway Trust Fund was scheduled to expire on that October 31, interim funding was provided.

With the Democrats divided and Republicans opposing the *Build Back Better* reconciliation bill and congressional action pending on an increase in the national debt limit, the White House had to intervene. The president, vice president, and senior aides held separate meetings with two dozen moderate and progressive Democrats for a span of five hours, with the president requesting that House moderates give him a spending figure they could support for the reconciliation package. He asked progressives to give him leeway to negotiate a deal, promised to support their goals although did not commit to their scope and cost, and said he would speak to their congressional leadership to work out a voting schedule to meet the contingencies of each side.

The frenetic activities ended the night of November 5. It was Friday when Biden was scheduled to return to his beach home in Rehobeth, Maryland. He canceled the trip, set up a war room in his residence in the White House, called moderates and progressives, and worked out a compromise with Speaker Pelosi on voting for the bipartisan infrastructure proposal that night. He even called into a heated discussion of the Congressional Progressive caucus to plead for his compromise and asked members to vote on the bill on November 5 and on his larger social spending bill later in the month. He assured progressives that moderates would do so as well.

Biden had finally abandoned his cautious approach with members of the House; his near total reliance on Pelosi and her leadership team had not produced a vote, much less a consensus. Tension between the White House and Congress had increased. Relations within the White House became tense. The president became short tempered. Enough was enough. Biden finally issued a public statement that all members of the House should vote for the bill that night (Friday), a message he refrained from uttering earlier when he spoke to the Democratic caucus before leaving for the climate conferences. Muscle had replaced the nice guy's soft-sell approach.[4] And it was successful. Six progressive Democrats deserted him and the Speaker, but Biden and Pelosi were able to gain the support of 13 Republicans. The final vote was 228 to 206. Biden scored his second major legislative victory. He ceremoniously signed the bill into law on November 15. (See Box 7.2 for its major provisions and costs.)

Sending the Senate-passed bill to the House was the next step.

Box 7.2 The Bipartisan Infrastructure Bill: Major Provisions and Costs

Transportation	New Spending (in billions of dollars)	Excluded From Bill
Roads and Bridges	110	Research and Development
Road Safety	11	Manufacturing Incentives
Airports	25	Housing, Schools, and Businesses
Railways	66	Clean Energy Tax Credit
Public Transit	39	Home- and Community-Based Care
Ports and Waterways	17	
Climate		
Electric Vehicles	15	
Clean Up Wells and Mines	17	
Resiliency	47	
Infrastructure		
Power-Electric Grid	65	
Water	55	
Broadband Expansion	65	
Miscellaneous	1	
Total New Spending	533	
Existing Highway Funds	450	
Total	**$1.03 trillion**	

The legislation that was finally enacted by Congress contained a multitude of special projects that the senators who negotiated the bill and the White House desired: money for Amtrak, the Washington DC Metro, a highway in Alaska, the restoration of various bodies of water, regional commissions, and underserved minority communities.[5] (See Box 7.1.)

In December, after an attempt by some Republican senators to delay appropriations to run the government until Biden's COVID mandates for the private sector were ended, a compromise was eventually reached to allow a vote on the mandate issue before voting on a resolution that would extend funding for the government until early February. The bill was signed into law on December 16, 2021.

Photo 7.1 *President Joe Biden signs the $1.2 trillion bipartisan infrastructure bill into law on November 15, 2021*
Source: AP Photo/Susan Walsh

The debt issue was mired in partisan differences. Republicans wanted the Democrats to do it through the reconciliation process and be tagged as the party that increased the debt, while Democrats wanted a bipartisan, share-the-blame vote. As the deadline neared when the Treasury would not have enough funds to repay the money borrowed, a compromise was reached in which there would be two separate roll-call votes, the first in which a sufficient number of Republicans would join the Democrats to raise the debt limit and the second in which Republicans would oppose the amount that the Democrats wanted to raise it, forcing the Democrats to use the reconciliation process to do so. The Republican leader, Mitch McConnell, also noted that raising the limit would be more difficult in subsequent years if they controlled one or both Houses of Congress.

Partial Success

Climate Change

Improving the environment was a key priority of the Biden administration and Democratic Congress. In a speech before the United Nations General

Assembly, Biden promised to reduce U.S. greenhouse gas emissions by 50 percent by 2030. Such a reduction would be costly, require the development of new technologies, create employment displacements, and continue the transition from an economy based on manufacturing to one based on information and services. Education would play a role as well, with the need for more training in science and technology. Gaps in education would produce greater income inequality. The changes would be massive and the short time span in which to achieve them difficult and disruptive.

Biden said the program would improve the environment, improve the health of the citizenry, create new jobs, and make the U.S. more competitive within the international community; Republicans were not so confident. Although Americans consider climate change an important issue, they do not consider it the most important problem facing the United States today. Only 3 to 5 percent believed it was.[6] Nonetheless, increasing heat, fires, floods, and hurricanes have kept the issue alive. On September 30, the president signed into law a bill that provided $28.6 billion in emergency relief to areas devastated by natural disasters. The funds were part of legislation designed to extend government operations until December 3, 2021, and provide emergency aid of $6.8 billion for the resettlement of Afghan refugees.

Republicans were less enthusiastic about the environmental issues and the warming climate. They were opposed to the costs of the legislation that Congress was considering, fearing that they would fuel inflation, raise the price of energy, impose more government restrictions on industries, and in the short run adversely affect U.S. competitiveness. Industry and labor unions also objected to increased costs and potential dislocation in gaining good-paying jobs. Critics also pointed out these U.S. policies would create problems between advanced and underdeveloped countries, which were dependent on their abundant supplies of fossil fuel that they needed to use, sell, and improve their standard of living. Underdeveloped countries pointed out that for years it was the United States and Western Europe that were the major industrial polluters and that disproportionately had contributed to the problem. Democratic Senator Joe Manchin from West Virginia, a coal-producing state, also objected to most of the fossil fuel restrictions, especially the financial penalties imposed on their atmospheric emissions, and federal subsidies for electric vehicles.

Nonetheless, Biden pursued his climate objectives with much fanfare in the new legislation he supported, especially the orders he gave to executive agencies to include climate considerations in their proposals, and the rules issued by the Environmental Protection Agency (EPA).[7] Following the president's promise to the international community to reduce greenhouse gases in the United States, the EPA issued a rule that cut hydrofluorocarbons, used in refrigerators, freezers, and air conditioners, by 85 percent. The rule implemented a 2020 congressional statute. The EPA has continued to issue rules reducing greenhouse gases as well as "forever chemicals" that do not break down naturally and may be found in drinking water. The EPA's authority to issue such rules, however, was challenged by coal companies and other fossil fuel producers. The supreme court ruled in June 2022 that the agency had overstepped its authority.

The bipartisan infrastructure bill also contained plans to reduce congestion at transportation centers such as airports and waterways, improve the efficiency and operations of the electric grid, and electrify cars, buses, and other means of public transportation with electric charging stations placed along all major interstate highways.

Items in the House's *Build Back Better Act* also provided $550 billion in federal funding for climate improvement to incentivize renewable energy sources, develop manufacturing technology, subsidize the purchase of electric cars, and retrofit buildings and apartments to enhance their resiliency, but the bill was not enacted into law.

Despite the public's view that climate change was real, supported by scientific evidence, and had to be addressed, increased energy costs, fear of job displacements in the fossil fuel industry, and the more advanced educational training required for developing and operating new renewable energy technologies, potentially advantaging opportunities for the more educated Caucasian population and decreasing those of less-educated minorities, remained points of contention. Additionally, gas-driven cars and trucks had become more reliable, safer, and fuel efficient, especially hybrid vehicles.

As a consequence, Biden did not get everything he wanted. Dropped from the original bill that the House enacted were financial incentives rewarding utilities for reducing their fossil fuels consumption, penalties on coal mining operations, plans for terminating government permits for off-shore drilling, and plans for reducing methane gas emissions.

The president tried to counter these omissions with executive actions that increased average mileage for automobiles and trucks by 2030, but the constitutionality of the EPA's rules on the environment was also in doubt; they were challenged by opponents in the courts.

Delays

Build Back Better Act

Climate control, educational expansion, and new and more generous social welfare programs, omitted from the bipartisan infrastructure bill, were the next policy issue that confronted Congress after it returned from its summer recess. Democrats planned to use the reconciliation process as a vehicle for enacting the legislation.

The size of the bill, its original estimated cost of $3.5 trillion, and the need for an increase in the Treasury's borrowing limit engendered partisan opposition as well as internal disagreements within the Democratic Party and between Democrats in the House and the Senate. These differences, especially within the party, required a massive White House effort to negotiate a bill that every Senate Democrat and almost every House Democrat would accept.

Reconciliation avoided the filibuster problem, but the components of the bill still required the approval of the Senate Parliamentarian and no Democratic defections. Would new emission standards, educational programs, and housing qualify as direct impacts on the budget? The defection issue gave moderate Democratic senators individual veto power over the contents of the legislation proposed by the House. The extent of the changes could jeopardize both *The American Rescue Plan Act of 2021* as well as House support for the bipartisan infrastructure bill. The White House had to engage in internal Democratic lobbying to find common and acceptable ground for a unified Democratic vote. There was also the question of increasing revenue proposals (taxes) as well as increased borrowing power for the Treasury Department. The debt limit authorization had lapsed on July 31 and government funding on September 30, two issues on which there was strong partisan disagreement. After much negotiation between Senate leaders, a short-term compromise was reached that extended government funding and the debt limit ceiling to December 3, 2021. The fight was not over.

The Biden administration had planned an extensive public campaign in the relatively slow news-making month of August when the president was on vacation and Congress was in recess. The purpose of the campaign was to gain news media attention and to inform the public and build support for what the president had done and was doing and for congressional passage of pending legislation. Cabinet members were scheduled to visit multiple cities in multiple states. Pro-Biden groups planned to spend $100 million during this period on an advertising campaign. Progressive organizations were to be particularly active, staging more than 1,000 events and activities to pressure Congress to act.

During the recess and after it, senior White House officials and liaison aides were heavily involved in internal communications and lobbying. With House progressives and liberals divided and two Democratic senators opposing parts of the mammoth reconciliation bill that expanded the safety net, contained new climate initiatives, and strengthened the health-care system, the president became engaged in the behind-the-scenes negotiations but not in the publicized aspects of the Democratic debate. Biden received multiple daily briefings from White House aides who were meeting with and talking to members of the House and Senate. During this period, he participated in ongoing sessions with his economic, domestic, and political advisors.

The president's style throughout the negotiations was not to threaten but to find common ground if a compromise were to be made that allowed both pieces of the legislation to become law.[8] He did not harangue; he talked endlessly with the two moderate senators who opposed a massive social spending bill and endlessly with progressives who favored one. He limited his public outreach and stayed close to the ongoing negotiations. It was his old senator style now dressed in presidential garb.

Biden's representatives on the Hill listened to members of Congress and their staffs and passed on information they received to the White House. Their job was not to persuade; that job was left to the leadership of Congress, the White House, and eventually the president. Biden met twice with the House Democratic Caucus on Capitol Hill, the last meeting on the day he was scheduled to travel to climate conferences in Europe and meet the Pope. In his remarks to the Democrats before leaving, the president indicated that the policies in the climate, social, and education bill were significant, and that they addressed many of the priorities his party was demanding, even though the price tag for Biden's plan was only about half the size of the previous Democratic proposal.

In his remark to the Democratic caucus, Biden made it clear that the fate of his presidency and the Democratic Party hung on the successful passage of both legislative proposals, the bipartisan infrastructure bill and the *Build Back Better Act*. Mike Donilon, one of the president's senior aides, backed up Biden's remarks on the political significance of the legislation for the Democratic Party in the 2022 midterm elections. The White House also indicated that excluded items would be considered again during his presidency.

On October 29, the president made the biggest gamble of his presidency. He left for Europe without a done deal but hoped, probably prayed, and expected one to be made after he returned to the United States the following week. More behind-the-scenes negotiations on timing and contents of the pending legislation continued among senior presidential aides, House committee chairs, and senators, especially between Joe Manchin (WV) and Kyrsten Sinema (AZ) who had indicated their concern with the cost of the legislation and revenue sources to pay for it.

The House finally enacted the *Build Back Better Act* on a partisan vote on November 19. The vote was preceded by an eight-hour and thirty-minute speech by House Minority Leader Kevin McCarthy, who used the time to slow the vote on the bill, criticize the Democrats' policy agenda, and appeal to fellow House Republicans. McCarthy hoped to be elected Speaker if the Republicans controlled the House after the 2022 midterm elections.

The bill next went to the Senate, where moderate Democrats were expected to trim the costs back and modify some of the proposals contained in the House's $2.2 trillion package. With the Christmas and New Year holiday break approaching, the House completing its first session, and the upper chamber consumed by other business, primarily confirmations, the legislation never reached the floor of the Senate. Not only had its Parliamentarian ruled that it could not be placed in a reconciliation bill, but two Democratic senators, Kyrsten Sinema (AZ) and Joe Manchin (WV), opposed some of the provisions and cost. Sinema objected to tax increases, while Manchin indicated that he did not support paid family leave, in addition to many of the environmental components of the House's bill.

To make matters worse, Senator Manchin was reportedly irritated by the White House ending its tacit agreement with him to keep considering his objections to the House bill and his suggestions for changing it, blaming him publicly for delaying the legislation.[9] Manchin indicated on a radio interview right before the Senate recessed that he would not be browbeaten into supporting the measure, thereby forcing the Democrats' majority leader to put off the legislation to the next session.[10] By then, the president also conceded that the bill had to be delayed.

House progressives, increasingly critical of the West Virginia Senator, directed their anger at him for the demise of the legislation in the first session of Congress. The liberal news media also emphasized his role in objecting to the House bill. Progressive Democrats who constituted a large majority of Speaker Pelosi's voting bloc urged the president to take executive actions to achieve some of the bill's objectives, but it was not clear what specific actions he could take.

Box 7.3 lists the major provisions and costs of the House-passed measure.

Box 7.3 **The *Build Back Better Act*: Provisions and Costs**

Provisions	Costs (in billions of dollars)
Climate	
Cleaner Energy and Climate Initiatives, Including:	$555
A Civilian Climate Corps	
Tax Credits for Use of Solar Panels	
Business Incentives to Improve the Efficiency of Wind Turbines	
Subsidies for the Purchase of Electric Cars	
Education	
Money for Childcare and Universal Pre-K (for kids three to four years old)	400
Extension of Childcare and	
Earned Income Tax Deduction	200
Increase in Pell Grants for Needy Students and Investment for Traditionally Black Colleges and Universities	40
Health Care	
Subsidies for the Affordable Care Act and Closing the Medicaid Gap	130
Expanded Hearing Coverage	35
Home Care for the Elderly and Disabled	150
Housing	
Rehabilitate Older Housing, Rental Assistance,	150
Help for First-Time Home Buyers, and Other Equity and Investments	90
Total	**$1.75 trillion**
Exclusions From the Bill	**Revenue Sources**
Paid Leave	15% Minimum Corporate Tax
No Negotiation Between Medicare on Drug Prices	Tax on Company Buyback of

No New Eye and Dental Coverage from Medicare	Stock
No Free Community College Tuition	5% Subtax Increase on People with Incomes Over $10 Million and an Additional 3% Subtax on Incomes Over $25 Million; Increase in IRS Investigation of Tax Dodgers

- Biden also added $100 million for immigration reform.

Voting Rights

Another contentious delayed legislative issue was national voting rights. To counter restrictions placed on voter access in Republican-controlled states, House Democrats had proposed two bills, the *For the People Act* and the *John R. Lewis Voting Advancement Rights Act*. The *For the People Act* eased, expanded, and automatized registration procedures; broadened the base of citizen eligibility, including incarcerated individuals convicted of misdemeanors; facilitated voting for the disabled; allowed for early voting, voting by mail, and the inclusion of provisional votes; reversed the Supreme Court's *Citizens United* (2010) decision; strengthened voting security by requiring a paper trail to verify machine and computer tabulations; and authorized the Election Assistance Commission to implement these changes. States were also required to establish independent commissions for redistricting. The *John R. Lewis Voting Advancement Rights Act* reestablished the Justice Department's ability to change or negate voting changes in states with a record of discriminatory practices that the Supreme Court's decision in *Shelby County v. Holder* (2013) restricted. The House bill made election day a federal holiday, required same-day registration for all the states, set minimum rules for mail-in voting, and banned partisan gerrymandering.

Republicans strongly opposed national voting rights legislation, claiming that it would allow the federal government to nullify state election laws in violation of the Constitution's provision to have the states conduct elections for federal officials, although the Constitution also gives Congress the power to enact legislation that alters state election laws. The partisan consequences of such legislation reinforced the political division with the filibuster rule still in place. The Democrats proposed exempting the rule for constitutional issues, but they lacked the votes to do so; Biden did not initially support exempting the rule for constitutional issues.

With the midterm elections looming, a favorable legislative outcome for the Democrats seemed out of reach. Outside pressure by pro-voting right groups[11] did not change the situation, although some Democrats thought that the failure to pass these laws might boost minority voting in the next election cycle.

In the end, the only viable alternative for the Democrats was to ask the Justice Department to challenge restrictive state voting laws, which the department did. The attorney general promised to protect voting rights, doubled the enforcement staff of his civil rights division, and worked with other federal agencies to prevent disinformation campaigns that discouraged people from registering and voting, but legal challenges take time to be resolved. Although the president spoke privately with some senators, at least two Democrats, in addition to all the Republicans, still opposed changing the unlimited debate rule on substantive legislative policy matters.

Immigration Reform

The U.S. Citizenship Act of 2021 was introduced in the House of Representatives on February 19, 2021. The bill provided a way to obtain citizenship for certain undocumented immigrants who had been continually present in the United States since January 1, 2021, and who had passed background checks. After a minimum of five years, an eligible noncitizen could apply for and receive permanent resident status. The legislation allows noncitizens who came to the United States as minors or agricultural workers, eligible for temporary protected status or deferred enforced departure on January 1, 2017, to apply.

The State Department, charged with implementing the legislation, would be required to design a plan to address immigration from Central America, and some Customs and Border Patrol agents would need to have paramedic training. The bill also authorizes federal funds for training and services to immigrants. The Congressional Budget estimated its cost for its first ten years at approximately $122 billion.

Legislative Failures

Evictions

The Centers for Disease Control and Prevention (CDC) had put a temporary ban on evictions through July 31, 2021, because of the coronavirus pandemic. Challenged in court, the Supreme Court upheld the ban, but Justice Brett Kavanaugh, voting with the majority, said that Congress had to reauthorize the ban; the executive branch could not do so on its own. Kavanaugh's admonition prompted the president's counsel to oppose an attempt by senior White House officials to persuade Biden to extend the ban. Two days before the House was scheduled to recess for the summer, the White House informed the Congress, specifically Speaker Pelosi, of the need for legislation to extend the moratorium on evictions, but there was not sufficient time to do so.

Speaker Pelosi was upset to be put in the position of rounding up a majority as Congress was recessing and being blamed for gutting the eviction moratorium if she could not reverse it through legislation. Progressive Democrats were furious, directing their anguish and criticism toward the White House. One member of the House who had been evicted from her home three times as a child staged a five-day sleep-in on the steps of the Capitol, which was joined by other progressive Democrats. The attention the matter received from the news media, the plight of renters being forced from their homes as the Delta variant of the virus spread, and the adverse impact on minorities and others who lost their jobs during the pandemic, prompted the president, after consulting with lawyers, to reverse his decision and approve a narrowing ban. He announced several days later that the CDC would extend the temporary ban for another 60 days in areas with "high levels of community transmission" of the coronavirus, which amounted to a significant portion of the country.

Opponents immediately initiated litigation to challenge the president's actions; the Justice Department issued a brief defending the temporary extension. The administration anticipated a legal battle over its action but hoped that the additional two months and public pressure would encourage cities and states to extend federal aid that Congress had approved ($47 billion), most of which had not been spent by the states at that time.

A federal judge and later a three-judge panel of the U.S. Court of Appeals ruled in favor of the extension, but the Supreme Court overruled it. On August 26, 2021, a 6 to 3 summary judgment stated that the

CDC lacked the authority to extend the emergency moratorium. Only Congress could do so. The ball was back in Pelosi's court as progressives and African Americans pressured her and Senate Majority Leader Chuck Schumer to initiate legislation to extend the eviction moratorium. They also urged President Biden to prioritize the matter.

The eviction controversy was an instance of delayed White House decision-making, an impossible legislative request, and as members of Congress saw it, blame shifting from the White House to Congress. It had the potential of affecting Democratic unity that the president needed for his major legislative priorities as well as incurring the wrath of a significant part of his party's electoral base. Faced with a "no-win" situation, the president chose time over a legal consensus as the basis for his decision. His heart had overruled his head,[12] but the Supreme Court reversed his actions. Nonetheless, in the weeks between the president's decision and the Supreme Court's ruling, states' distribution of federal rental assistance increased.[13]

Police Reform

The group of House and Senate representatives negotiating police reform failed to reach agreement. Republicans accused Democrats of trying to defund the police, while Democrats charged that the Republicans were insensitive to discriminatory unlawful arrest practices. They also objected to the limited liability that protected police against criminal and civil suits by victims who were the subject of police abuse and illegal arrests, restrictions on the use of deadly force, and a national database of police misconduct.

The focus on Biden's three principal legislative priorities, *The American Rescue Act of 2021*, the bipartisan infrastructure bill, and the *Build Back Better Act* delayed consideration of other issues: background checks for gun purchases, the legalization of undocumented immigrants, policing reforms, and qualified immunity for law enforcement officers accused of misconduct.[14]

Other Legislation

Helping American Victims Afflicted by Neurological Attacks (HAVANA) Act of 2021

The bill, also known as the *Havana Act* because the first such incidents occurred in Cuba, provides services for U.S. (HAVANA) officials whose mental health was affected by these "attacks."

National Defense Authorization Act for the Fiscal Year 2022

This bill does *not* repeal authorization for the 2003 resolution allowing President George W. Bush to use military force against Iraq, require private sector companies to report incidents of hacking to the government, or include women in the draft. It *does* provide more protections against sexual assault and related crimes involving military personnel outside the chain of command, except in cases of a court martial, and it creates an independent commission to evaluate lessons of the Afghanistan war. The estimated cost of this enactment is $768 billion, $25 billion more than Biden requested.[15]

Congressiona Appropriations Act of 2022

The legislation provides supplemental appropriations for the fiscal year of 2022.

Emmitt Till AntiLyching Act

This law makes lynching a federal offense punishable by fine or a jail term of up to 30 years.

Postal Reform Act of 2022

This bill reforms the operations and finances of the United States Postal Service.

Ending the Importation of Russian Oil Act

This law bans the importation of energy products from Russia.

Suspending Normal Trade Relations with Russia and Belarus Act

This law allows the president to impose property and visa sanctions on violators of human rights in these countries.

Access to Baby Formula Act of 2022

This legislation authorizes the Agriculture Department to address the shortage of baby formula in the United States.

Open Shipping Reform Act of 2022

This bill gives the Federal Maritime Commission authority to investigate and penalize international carriers that enter U.S. territorial waters and charge excessive fees for shipping.

Bipartisan Safer Communities Act of 2022

The first gun law to pass and be enacted in two decades, this act strengthens and expands background checks for purchasers of firearms but does not ban assault weapons.

Political Repercussions of the Legislative Struggle

Internal Democratic disagreements dominated the news. The public story was about factional conflict within the party among people, ideas, and actual proposals. The Democrats' loss of the Virginia governor's election in early November added to the party's troubled perceptions. Failure to enact the legislation was not an option. Too much was at stake for the Democratic Party and the president. His popularity and reputation already had been damaged. Democrats were trailing Republicans in generic surveys for the 2022 midterm election.

Biden's job support eroded. By mid-October, only 36 percent approved his handling of the situation, and 41 percent disapproved, with the remaining having no opinion and little knowledge about of the internal party debate. Even though the Republicans were basically excluded from the House's deliberations, their party's handling of the controversy dropped as well, with only 18 percent approving their handling of the situation. Their criticisms concerning excessive cost, new taxes to pay for it, and the enlargement of the welfare state did not engage or enlarge public debate.[16]

From the perspective of most Americans, the major issues in the new proposals were health care and education; childcare and family leave programs were not as high on their list of priorities.

It was a tough period for Biden. Next to COVID and economic recovery, the Democratic divisions over these two legislative priorities, the bipartisan infrastructure proposal and *Build Back Better Act*, were the most serious political problems he faced during his first year in office. They took too long to resolve, with the news media describing the Democrats' conflicting priorities as internal factional divisions. Biden mediated but did not command, giving the impression that he was not in control of events. He evidenced patience but was slow to persuade. Americans were reminded of the dysfunctional presidential–congressional relations of previous administrations.

A Legislative Balance Sheet

Before Congress recessed for August, Biden signed into law just 12 legislative measures, only one of which was a major policy initiative. By the end of his first year, 81 bills were enacted into law, only two of which were major policy initiatives; by July 19, 2022 that number increased to 159. (Table 7.1 lists the total number of laws and vetoes during the first calendar year of recent presidents.)

Nominations and Confirmations

The pace of confirmations of presidential nominations also continued to remain very slow. For the top 806 top politically-appointed positions in the executive branch, only 556 were nominated and 400 were confirmed by July 19, 2022.[17] (See Table 7.2 for comparative data on nominations and confirmations of recent presidents at the end of their first year in office.)

TABLE 7.1 Legislation Enacted into Law and Vetoed

President	Public Laws	Vetoed
Biden	81	0
Trump	115	0
Obama	169	0
George W. Bush	133	0
Clinton	210	11 (one of which was overridden)
Total	708	11

Source: "Public Laws," 117th Congress

TABLE 7.2 Nominations and Confirmations

President	Nominated	Confirmed	
Biden	88	55	(55%)
Trump	53	47	(75%)
Obama	107	91	(85%)
George W. Bush	115	103	(90%)

Source: "Joe Biden's First Year in Office: Nominations and Confirmations," Center of Presidential Transition of the Partnership of Public Service

Notes

1. Alex Gangitano and Morgan Chalfant, "Biden Says He Won't Sign Bipartisan Bill Without Reconciliation Bill," *The Hill*, June 24, 2021.
2. Joe Biden, "Statement by President Joe Biden on the Bipartisan Infrastructure Framework," *White House*, June 26, 2021.
3. "Biden Loses Ground With the Public on Issues, Personal Traits and Job Approval," *Pew Research Center*, September 23, 2021.
4. Sean Sullivan, Marianna Sotomayor, and Tyler Pager, "Biden Gets Infrastructure Package Across Finish Line," *Washington Post*, November 7, 2021.
5. Emily Cochtane, Christopher Flavelle, and Alan Rappaport, "$1 Trillion Infrastructure Bill Pours Money Into Long Delayed Needs," *New York Times*, August 4, 2021.
6. "Topics A–Z: Most Important Problem," *Gallup Poll*, July–September, 2021.
7. Lauren Egan, "Biden Administration Releases Alarming Report on Climate Change," *NBC News*, October 7, 2021.
8. Jeff Stein and Seung Min Kim, "Biden Is Under a Deadline Crunch," *Washington Post*, October 10, 2021.
9. Steve Clemons, "White House Incivility Is What 'Lost' Joe Manchin," *The Hill*, December 20, 2021.
10. Manchin had been informed by the White House that his opposition to the bill would be publicly criticized. He requested that his name not be included in the official critical commentary because his family had been the target of abuse and threats. Nonetheless, he was personally mentioned. Irritated and angered, he expressed his discontent two days later. Biden called him that night to apologize and to say that he had not been consulted about the final draft and disagreed with its contention that White House and Manchin's negotiations were over.
11. These groups spent more than $150 million in the first six months of 2021 on voting rights and other issues. Ariel Gans, "Push for Voting Rights Pulls in Big Money," *Opensecrets.org*, October 5, 2021.

12. For an excellent discussion of the eviction decision-making, see Michael D. Shear, Glenn Thrush, Charlie Savage, and Alan Rappaport, "As Democrats Seethed, White House Struggled to Contain Eviction Fallout," *New York Times*, August 7, 2021.

13. "More than 420,000 Households Received Emergency Rental Assistance in August, Totaling Over $2.3 Billion in Payments," *United States Treasury*, September 24, 2021.

14. Qualified immunity protects police and government in general from civil suits. It puts the burden of proof on those who claim that their constitutional rights were violated by public officials, such as the police.

15. Karoun Demirjain, "$768 Billion Defense Bill Is Approved," *Washington Post*, December 16, 2021.

16. Kevin Freking and Hannah Fingerhut, "Biden, Dems Get Low Marks on Spending Tasks," *AP-NORC Poll*, October 28, 2021.

17. *Partnership for Public Service*, July 20, 2022.

CHAPTER 8
THE BIDEN WHITE HOUSE

The size of the executive branch, 15 departments, 270 executive agencies, 67 independent agencies, and more than 40 boards, commissions, and committees staffed by approximately 2.1 million people, creates a significant management challenge for the president, especially when something goes wrong and becomes public. Moreover, many of the implementation issues require interagency cooperation and coordination in order for the administration to speak with a single voice and pursue a common strategy.

Creating a Presidential Organization

The expansion of the executive branch during Roosevelt's New Deal magnified the management problem presidents face today. To counter charges that he was administering the government poorly, Roosevelt proposed that Congress give him authority to create an Executive Office of the President (EOP) to support increasing demands on the presidency and its oversight of the government. Congress did so in 1939. The composition of the EOP has expanded and changed over the years. Roosevelt began with five separate units, including a White House office and a Bureau of the Budget. Biden's EOP consists of 13 offices staffed by a total of approximately 1,900 people with a budget of $476 million. (See Table 8.1).

Structure and Personnel

The White House is the focal point for presidential statements, decisions, and actions. It is the chief policymaking, policy-promoting, and

TABLE 8.1 The Executive Office of the President

Offices	Number of Full-Time Employees (FTEs)	Budget for FY 2022 (in millions of dollars)
Council of Economic Advisors	28	5
Council on Environmental Quality	22	4
National Cyber Security	25	15
National Security Council (includes Homeland Security Council)	72	13
National Space Council	7	2
Office of Administration	245	111
Office of Management and Budget	516	122
Office of National Drug Control Policy	72	21
Office of Science and Technology Policy	37	7
Office of U.S. Trade Representative	244	58
Trust Fund Management	36	15
Vice President's Office and Residence	27	6
White House Office (includes Domestic, Gender, and Economic Councils, Intergovernmental Affairs, Public Engagement, and other units)	471	80
Presidential Residence	98	15
Unanticipated Needs	7	2
Total	**1,907**	**476**

crisis management body. Traditionally, about 400 people are on the White House budget that is submitted to Congress. Biden's White House is larger with about 560 senior, junior, and secretarial and support staff working there on an ongoing basis. The White House claimed that the increase in personnel was needed to cope with the magnitude of the problems the president faced when he was first elected; including the pandemic and its economic impact, hacking and cybersecurity, racial, ethnic, and income inequities, and the need to form a commission to study the improvement and possible expansion of the federal judiciary. The slowness of the confirmation process and Biden's desire to centralize authority and outreach activities contributed as well. (See Table 2.1 for the organization of the initial Biden White House and the names of its senior staff.)

White House appointees do not require Senate confirmation, unlike most of the top executive branch jobs. The Partnership for Public Service, a nonpartisan think tank focusing on the operation of government, designated 806 top positions as requiring Senate confirmation. Only 11 percent of them had confirmed appointees in place at the end of Biden's first six months in office; as noted in the previous chapter, 556 had been nominated and 400 confimed by July 19, 2022; the rest of the positions were vacant without a designated nominee.[1]

Biden predecessors benefited from a speedier process, although confirmation has been slowed by the increase in the number of political appointments, the partisan polarization of the Senate, and the time-consuming process of vetting and then deciding on candidates for jobs with considerable political clout in particular policy areas.

Within the White House, there is a hierarchy of titles with assistants to the president, deputy assistants, and special assistants at the top of the pecking order. Assistants have the highest salaries, offices in the West Wing, and the most access to the president. Having a first-floor office in the West Wing is the most prestigious location. Other White House personnel are located in the East Wing, the Eisenhower Executive Office Building, which is next to the White House, and various offices in and around Lafayette Park.

Biden initially appointed 21 aides as senior staff, a larger number than his predecessors. More than half of those senior advisors were women. The composition of the entire White House was more diverse than previous White Houses, both Democratic and Republican. More than half of Biden's entire White House was composed of women (60 percent), and almost half were ethnic and racial minorities (44 percent).[2] But the president also tended to choose people who were educated at elite institutions; 41 percent had Ivy League degrees.[3]

Additionally, many of Biden's choices for his principal aides had served in previous Democratic White Houses, knew the president personally, worked with him in the Senate or as vice president, and helped him formulate his goals, strategy, and outreach during the 2020 campaign and transition. Some were longtime friends. Some junior staff were not friends and grew unhappy with the insular relationships among the top-heavy senior staff; many were not invited to celebratory events attended by members of Congress, their principal aides, and influential lobbyists. They complained that there was no team-building, only long hours and hard work. Plans to resign after one year were leaked to *Politico*'s reporters who covered the White House.[4]

The organization of the Biden White House followed standard divisions, conforming to others in the 21st century. As communication technology changed and people got their information from online sources, new offices extended presidential outreach. Table 8.2 lists the structure of the principal offices in the 2021 Biden White House.

Ron Klain, Biden's chief of staff, had previously headed two vice presidents' staffs, Al Gore's from 1995 to 1999 and Biden's from 2009 to 2011. He controlled the door to the Oval Office and the flow of information to the president; kept the White House focused on key presidential issues; communicated privately with members of Congress, particularly progressives; tweeted regularly with the press and party leaders; and was viewed as an accessible, friendly, and multifaceted chief. Klain also walled off the president's family, with the exception of the First Lady, from presidential decision-making, in contrast to the role some of Trump's children played in his administration.[5]

Three of the other major senior advisors, Bruce Reed, Mike Donilon, and Steve Ricchetti, exercised somewhat overlapping functions, but each had a particular sphere of influence. Reed, one of two deputy chiefs, had served in the Clinton White House, served on the Commission on Fiscal Responsibility and Reform that Obama created, and succeeded Klain as Vice President Biden's chief of staff in 2011. Reed concentrated on major domestic policies. The other deputy chief of staff, Jen O'Malley

TABLE 8.2 The Contemporary White House

First Lady	President	Vice President
Senior Advisors and Counselors	Chief of Staff (COS)	COVID-19 Advisor
	Deputy COS	Deputy COS
	Cabinet Secretary	
Outreach Offices	**White House Operations**	**Policy Offices**
Communications	Counsel	Domestic Climate
Digital Strategy	Management and Administration	Domestic Policy
Intergovernmental Affairs	Oval Office Operations	Economic Policy
Legislative Affairs	Personnel	Homeland Security
Political Strategy and Outreach	Scheduling and Advance	National Security
Press Secretary	Staff Secretary	Science Policy
Public Engagement	Social Secretary	
	Speech Writing	

Photo 8.1 *Ron Klain, Biden's Chief of Staff*
Source: Olivier Douliery/Abaca/Sipa USA

Dillon, managed Biden's 2020 campaign. Responsible for political matters, she was a principal White House link to the Democratic National
Committee and state party leaders. Dillon also coordinated major White
House policy initiatives with the executive department and agencies and
helped plan the president's public events. Other outreach officials include
former congressman Cedric Richmond, who headed the Office of Public
Engagement and managed interchange between outside groups and the
White House; Jen Psaki, Biden's first press secretary; and Kate Bedingfield, the communications director in charge of messaging.

Anita Dunn and Neera Tanden, both senior advisors, had varying
coordination responsibilities. After Biden's staff secretary announced she
was resigning, Tanden was given those responsibilities as well.

The senior White House staff with the title of "Assistant to the
President" are paid a maximum salary of $180,000. The president's sal-
ary is $400,000 plus a $50,000 expense budget; The vice president's
salary is $235,100 plus amenities.

Biden's two closest friends and longtime associates, Steve Ricchetti
and Tom Donilon, are senior advisors. Ricchetti focuses primarily on
policy and Congress, while Donilon concentrates on politics, public
opinion, presidential speeches, and White House messaging. Referred to
as "the Historians," Klain, Reed, Ricchetti, and Donilon participate in
most of the president's major decision-making meetings.[6]

Operating Style

The president's day was well-scripted, and Biden stuck to it. Unplanned activities, off-the-cuff remarks, and personal tweets by the president were initially few in number. Biden's White House operation was purposefully designed to contrast with Trump's, as were the president's personal behavior and professional activities in office.

Trump was a dominant decision maker. Impulsive, adamant, even vitriolic, he did not admit error. He sought confirmation and occasionally advice from longtime associates, his adult children, and aides who demonstrated their constant loyalty to him. Critics were castigated and ridiculed, especially when their negative comments became public. A quick decision maker, Trump had little patience for extended study and detailed expert knowledge. His judgments were often guided by an economic calculus, popular support from his political base, and his elevated stature as a strong and decisive leader.

Trump watched a lot of television and relied on friendly commentators to confirm his political and policy decisions. Staying front and center in the public arena, he believed, reinforced his power, prestige, and leadership. Tweets indicating his views, passions, and aggressive emotions were amplified online, elevating perceptions of himself and others. He reacted strongly and personally to negative criticism.

Biden, in contrast, presented a more thoughtful style and a much less pompous, self-promoting manner. He demonstrated his empathy, tolerance, and friendliness as a get-along-guy. His nature and experience inclined him toward moderation, consensus building, and personal relationships with those around him. He believed such relationships were key to achieving and maintaining a functional government in a diverse and highly discordant democratic society.

Biden was more deliberative than Trump, and more detail oriented, but no less opinionated. His almost 50 years in government had coalesced his policy views, their political ramifications, and his negotiating style. Moreover, after a campaign for the presidency in 1992 when his credentials, speech authorship, and intellect were questioned, and after a vice presidency in which his long-winded remarks and foreign policy judgments were criticized by other Obama policy advisors, and his tendency to veer off course was considered a major liability, Biden was determined to improve and firm up his public image.[7]

As president, he demonstrated resolve and confidence in his policy judgments. His staff drafted his speeches, limited his initial press contacts, orchestrated a comprehensive outreach program, kept lines of communication to and from the White House open, and scheduled his days to coincide with a planned, presidential announcement or action. Unanticipated events, such as the surge of immigrants seeking asylum at the southern border, the spread of the Delta variant of the COVID virus across the country, and the chaotic exodus from Afghanistan, took time to fashion a presidential response and public relations campaign.

From the outset, the Biden White House was well-disciplined and well-focused. Top-down management coordinated and controlled staff assignments. Turf fights were minimized and kept behind the scenes. Embarrassing leaks were minimized; purposeful leaks were permitted. Dutiful POTUS tweets were written by communication advisors.

Background statements from White House officials required approval before they could be released, a practice to which the news media strongly objected. The communications staff decided on which top officials would be made available to the press, when, and for how long. Personal contacts with the president and vice president required approval from their respective chiefs of staff.

As the administration progressed, however, Biden occasionally went off-message; feeling comfortable as president, allowing his strong feelings to surface in his public statements, he ad-libbed and sometimes got into trouble. His conflicting comments on signing the *Bipartisan Infrastructure* bill and Facebook reference to how COVID misinformation "kills people" are two early examples; his comments on the defense of Taiwan against a possible invasion by China is another.

White House turnover during Biden's first year was much less than Trump's. A few senior aides who indicated that they had only planned to serve for a few months left, and there were some quiet dismissals of lower-level personnel. The main culprit for the departures of junior staffers was their previous use of marijuana, identified in security checks. Smoking marijuana in the White House is a no-no. In addition, one public relations official who had threatened a reporter with reprisals if she revealed a personal relationship in which he was involved also submitted his resignation after his threat became public.

In his second year, turnover increased. By July 19, 2022, more than 25 percent of the senior EOP officials had left, but no cabinet secretaries.

Long hours, low wages and low morale were the principal factors that contributed to what was referred to as "the Great Resignation."

Ethical Considerations

Self-interest issues were also raised as they had been in previous administrations. After a controversy arose about Biden's son, Hunter, and his involvement with a Ukrainian company during Trump's first impeachment trial, Biden said that no member of his family would profit from his presidency, but family members of some of his senior White House aides have. The brother of one of the president's senior advisors heads a high-powered lobbying firm and represented General Motors during the infrastructure debate. The White House said that he could not lobby presidential aides on that issue. Other Democratic lobbyists who had worked for Biden in the past and on his campaign also benefited from the expansion of their clientele and their contacts with the administration. Nonetheless, the ethical code to which Biden's political appointees had to subscribe prohibited them from participating on any issue in which they had been involved for two years before joining and after leaving the government. Waivers were given, however, to those who worked for nonprofit groups.

There were other issues. Three children of one of the president's senior advisors were hired for middle- and low-level executive branch positions; a fourth worked on Capitol Hill for a Democratic member of Congress. The brother of another senior advisor saw his private-sector firm's lobbying revenues increase substantially. The White House denied that such employment and lobbying violated the new ethical rules of the Biden administration. Eyebrows were also raised, and ethical considerations were debated when the prices of some of Hunter Biden's paintings, put on sale by a New York art dealer, were revealed.

As candidate and president-elect, Biden had also pledged truth and transparency in his White House. He said that he would release logs of White House visitors as Obama had done but Trump had not. The latter cited national security concerns as the reason. Since many meetings with outsiders had to be conducted virtually during the pandemic, the press also requested the names of participants in those meetings. Although the Biden White House released a "read-out" of the discussion, it did not reveal the identities of those who attended online or visitors to the president's residence, but it did release the names of people who visited offices in the White House. Biden did not continue the petition process that President Obama had initiated in which a portal on the White House website encouraged the public to identify issues they wanted the president to address. Petitions signed by 100,000 people received a White House response within 30 days.

A 14-page guideline was issued by the president's legal counsel on the subject of how departments and agencies should communicate with each another. Biden wanted to avoid the perception of undue political pressures being placed on the departments and agencies by the White House, pressures that were alleged in the Trump administration.

The President's Day

The president began his Oval Office workday between 9 and 9:30 a.m. after exercising and breakfasting while reading the early morning news "Bulletin" prepared by his press aides.[8] He also continued reading *The News Journal*, a Delaware newspaper, every day. Knowing that he did so, policy advocacy groups began advertising in it to gain his attention. Although not a regular television viewer, Biden did watches the early morning news shows on CNN and MSNBC while exercising, although most of his knowledge of news coverage comes from the early morning news synopsis he received.[9]

The president usually began his Oval Office activities with an intelligence briefing that Vice President Harris usually attended. Meetings with staff and policy advisors followed, starting around 10 a.m. with 15-minute breaks scheduled between them in case they exceeded the time allotted for the session, a frequent occurrence when the president participated. With the exception of a 30-minute lunch, the workday continued until 6 to 7 p.m., when Biden returned to the residence for dinner with his wife and sometimes other family members. The president's nights were spent communicating with aides, friends, and family, reviewing mail that his correspondence staff compiled, and reading books, generally nonfiction. Few public events were planned for the weekends, which the president and his wife usually spend at their home in Delaware or at Camp David in Maryland. As a consequence, Sunday and Monday were slow domestic news days.

In making decisions, the president was reputed to be a stickler for details. A deliberative thinker, he did not rush to judgment. Normally, President Biden is calm, cautious, and slow to anger. When examining policy options, the president demands that a multitude of views be presented. He tends to concentrate on major issues and does not get bogged down on day-to-day newsworthy happenings, although he may have to address a current event.

Biden's White House has sometimes been criticized for its slow reaction to new situations that command public attention. Examples include the hacking of the Colonial Pipeline and shortage of gas on the East Coast; the Hamas–Israeli confrontation; anti-Asian, anti-Black, and anti-Semitic incidents; and even the CDC's surprise announcement on the unmasking of fully vaccinated individuals. Composed primarily of people who knew one another and who had worked together in the past, the White House decision-making team was also prone to and accused of a "groupthink" mentality. The Afghanistan pullout is a case in point.

The White House scheduled daily press conferences; provided in-depth briefings to reporters; and distributed readouts of major policy decisions and executive actions on its website along with fact sheets to support them. Again, the contrast with Trump was intentional, designed to show a hard-working but not self-promoting President Biden who determined and promoted his major policy initiatives and legislative successes. (See Chapter 13.)

The Harris Vice Presidency

Vice presidential candidates tend to receive more attention during their campaign for the office than as occupants in it, except during periods of presidential health emergencies or when they succeed in resolving a critical issue. As candidates, they speak and act in the public arena, praising their presidential running mate and the achievements they will accomplish together. As vice presidents, however, they defer to the president, tend to remain behind the scenes except in the case of a well-publicized photograph showing them working, meeting with important foreign leaders, or taking credit for achieving one of the administration's goals. Within the White House, they are seen and sometimes heard, but outside it, most people do not view them as influential policy makers. Rather, they are seen doing the president's bidding in public events that the president cannot or does not want to attend. Funerals are a good example.

Other than succeeding to the office if the president dies, resigns, or is impeached, their only constitutionally designated function is to preside over the Senate as its president and vote in case of a tie. Vice President Harris cast 23 tie-breaking votes in her first 18 months in office. Other than casting the tie-breaking vote, the vice president has little power to affect Senate rules and procedures, to which Vice President Pence attested when he told President Trump that he did not have the constitutional authority to affect the certification of the electoral vote count of the 2020 presidential election.

Even succession to the presidency was not a certainty until precedent was established when John Tyler, the first vice president to succeed to the office, rushed to Washington upon the death of President William Henry Harrison to demonstrate his right to the office. Tyler feared that he might still be considered vice president and only act in a presidential capacity without his predecessor's salary and authority. It was not until the ratification of the Twenty-Fifth Amendment in 1967 that the vice president's position was clarified during periods of presidential disability, demise, resignation, or impeachment. That amendment also specifies procedures for temporarily or permanently assuming the authority of the president and also for filling the vice presidency if it becomes vacant.

Prior to the Jimmy Carter presidency, vice presidents performed limited roles and exercised minimum power. They did not even have an office in the West Wing of the White House. The closest they got was a first-floor office in the Executive Office Building next to the White House, separated by a public road.

Most vice presidential candidates were chosen as running mates, not governing mates. Carter selected Walter Mondale for his experience, knowledge of Washington, and willingness to articulate his opinion in private discussions with Carter, who involved Mondale in decision-making and gave him a West Wing office on the same floor as the president's.

Presidents who followed Carter usually said that they would follow the Mondale model when choosing and using their vice presidents, and most did. Al Gore, Dick Cheney, and Joe Biden were active participants in their administrations' most important policy decisions. Biden announced that Kamala Harris would perform a similar role in his administration as an advisor, advocate, and outreach to minority communities. She regularly participated in policy discussions, presidential briefings, and public events. During the first four months of the Biden presidency, the pandemic kept them together for much of the day.

In addition to helping to shape policy within the White House, Harris communicated with foreign leaders and met with outside groups interested in any given issue under consideration. Biden wanted Harris's voice to be heard. He was particularly supportive of her concern about inclusiveness and inequities, her appeal to and credibility with minority groups, and her analytical skills as a prosecuting attorney.

Like Biden, Harris follows the White House schedule and script. Her aides have been careful not to try to elevate her influence within the White House. Presidential loyalty has been her most important attribute.

As the first woman and first woman of color to hold that office, Harris has faced high public expectations, which have generated considerable attention from the press, her minority constituencies, and Republicans. Her potential to succeed the president, given his age, the uncertainty whether he would seek reelection, and the advantage that vice presidents have had in winning their party's nomination, have increased the focus on Harris's potential political ambitions but thus far have not enhanced her stature as a future electable Democratic nominee as much as her supporters would like.

Meeting leadership expectations from a position of followership is difficult. Loyalty to the president requires vice presidents not to take attention or credit away from the president. Both Biden and Pence as vice presidents performed assigned roles rather than initiated them on their own.

There have also been tensions within Harris's staff and with the White House. She has had relatively high turnover of senior aides, including two communication experts who were added to her staff to enhance her visibility and public messaging. Unlike President Biden who staffed the White House with people he had worked with in the past, Harris began her vice presidency with only two aides who had worked with her previously. Most of the vice president's staff were recommended by the White House. Some of the people who worked for the vice president complained that Harris was very demanding and occasionally demeaning.[10] The news media highlighted these staffing issues.

Harris has also been criticized for being overly cautious in her public statements and outreach activities. The Biden White House has been criticized for not giving her assignments that enhance her visibility and leadership skills.

During the first year of the Biden administration, Harris was charged with helping to stem the immigration surge at the southern border by engaging diplomatically with Mexico and the heads of the three Latin American countries from which many of the refugees came. Such negotiations did not produce a major reduction in immigration from the south, and she has been harshly criticized by Republicans for not initially visiting the southern border. Progressive Democrats even objected to her discouraging immigration from Central America.[11]

In August, the vice president was given a mission of meeting with leaders in Southeast Asia to emphasize America's concern for them, build economic ties that would strengthen competition with China, and engage in a variety of common issues such as addressing the COVID pandemic and harmful environmental change. Although these tasks were intended to enhance Harris's stature as an international spokesperson, they have not yet done so, in part because of the difficulty of the vice president achieving tangible results. The vice president was also asked to lead the fight for voting rights in the Senate and around the country, but she has been unable to overcome Republican opposition at the national and state levels. She was charged with chairing the National Space Council but did not call a meeting of the council until the first day of December.

Recently, the only vice presidents to be elected president have been Richard Nixon, George H. W. Bush, and Joe Biden, after four years of Republican control of the White House. Most vice presidents, however, have been able to obtain their party's nomination when the incumbent does not or cannot run for reelection.

Vice President Harris's office structure parallels the president's, although it is much smaller in size and scope. Headed by a chief of staff, Harris is aided by about 40 domestic, economic, and national security advisors, communications specialists and outreach personnel, a press secretary, speech writers, and others to advance her public trips and events. A photographer is also assigned to the vice president. Table 8.3 notes the principal positions.

The First Lady and Second Gentleman

Dr. Jill Biden has been an active and visible First Lady. An author, educator, and advocate for military families, cancer research, and community education, she regularly speaks on these initiatives as well as travels to White House scheduled events and rallies. Dr. Biden also maintains an academic position, teaching writing at a nearby community college.

A staff for the First Lady was initially created in 1977 to facilitate her social role and increasing public activities. First ladies gain more attention as presidential surrogates and advocates for social causes; their staffs expanded as well to include communication experts, social secretaries,

Table 8.3 The Vice President's Staff

Vice President
Chief of Staff (COS)
Deputy COS

Outreach	White House Operations	Policy Advisors
Communications	Counsel	National Security
Senior Advisor and Chief Spokesperson		Domestic
Speechwriting	Scheduling	Economic
Public Engagement and Intergovernmental Affairs		
Research	Staff Secretary	
Legislative Affairs	Management and Administration	
	Social Secretary	

Comparative Capsule 8.1   Organization and Personnel

BIDEN	TRUMP
Planned for a White House staff of 471	Planned for a White House staff of 408
Appointed gender, ethnic, and racial minorities to White House	Appointed mostly white males to White House
Vice President's race and electability newsworthy	Vice President's race and electability not as newsworthy
First Lady involved in promoting presidential priorities	First Lady primarily involved in official social events

and even political advisors. Dr. Biden has a staff of 14. Her first chief of staff, Julissa Reynoso, was nominated to be ambassador to Spain in July; Tina Flournoy replaced her in that position. Another important senior advisor to the First Lady, Anthony Bernal, plans her events, speeches, and other activities. His direct, often blunt style, however, has elicited some negative reactions from others on her staff.[12] The First Lady's office also includes a press secretary, social secretary, and floral designer to help Dr. Biden oversee the White House residence and food preparation.

Personnel who work directly for the First Lady have traditionally had their offices in the East Wing of the White House, although Hillary Clinton also had a West Wing office for her work on health care reform.

Mrs. Harris's husband, Doug Emhoff, the Second Gentleman, has an even smaller staff that is focused on his public activities. Vice presidential spouses are also allowed to work for compensation outside of their public responsibilities. They are not paid by the government but live in the vice president's mansion at the Naval Observatory. Mr. Emhoff, a lawyer, teaches a course in entertainment law at Georgetown Law School.

Notes

1. "Biden's Appointee Political Tracker," *Partnership for Public Service*, accessed June 20, 2021.
2. Alex Thompson, Tina Sfondeles, and Theodoric Meyer, "Biden's Bloated White House," *Politico*, July 1, 2021.
3. Mike Allen, "Exclusive Data: Biden Staffing Makes History," *Axios*, April 25, 2021.
4. Alex Thompson, Tina Sfondeles, and Max Tani, "Biden Aides Catch the Holiday Blues," *Politico: West Wing Playbook*, December 22, 2021.
5. Natasha Korecki and Daniel Lippman, "Inside Biden's Bubble: How an Insular White House Has Kept Drama and Leaks to a Minimum," *Politico*, April 27, 2021.
6. Michael D. Shear, Katie Rogers, and Annie Kurni, "Beneath Folksy Demeanor: A Deliberative Biden," *New York Times*, May 15, 2021.
7. Ryan Lizza, Rachel Bade, Eugene Daniels, and Tara Palmeri, "Biden's Stubborn Streak Paved the Way for Havoc in Afghanistan, Playbook," *Politico*, August 16, 2021.
8. Ashley Parker, "Biden's Typical Day Is Full of Routines and Little Escapes," *Washington Post*, May 26, 2021.
9. Hailey Fuchs and Max Tani, "How a 100-Year-Old Newspaper Became the Go-To Way to Influence Biden," *Politico*, December 14, 2021.
10. Cleve R. Wootson Jr. and Tyler Pager, "Harris Staff Exodus Reignites Leadership Concerns," *Washington Post*, December 4, 2021.
11. The Biden strategy, which the vice president was trying to implement, was to provide financial aid to nongovernmental organizations in Guatemala, Honduras, and El Salvador to improve the conditions that encouraged immigration. Harris's first international travel in June was to Mexico and Guatemala.
12. Alex Thompson and Tina Sfondeles, "West Wing Playbook," *Politico*, August 2, 2021.

CHAPTER 9
BIDEN AS CHIEF EXECUTIVE

The Constitution vests the executive power in the president. Being chief executive in theory, however, does not give the president operational control in practice. The size and complexity of the executive branch, Senate confirmation of its principal appointees, the nonpolitical, merit-based civil service system, and constraints of time, expertise, and operational knowledge of day-to-day activities plus agencies' standard operating procedures reduce ongoing White House influence on and oversight of executive branch decision-making unless important administrative priorities are involved. Similarly, the lack of extensive press coverage of most departments and agencies and the general public's very limited knowledge and interest in routine government operations, unless controversial decisions are made and publicized or scandals emerge, reduce the White House's incentive to stay deeply involved in executive branch decision-making, making the president the chief but not a hands-on manager.

Principles

Nonetheless, for Biden, restoring the public's trust in government and confidence in its operation was a principal objective for him; improving morale in the civil service was another. Unlike his predecessor, Biden did not fear what Trump called "the deep state." He saw government, especially at the federal level, as a positive force that could benefit the entire country rather than just influential groups and individuals.

Promoting equity was also a major objective of the new administration. Biden believed that the federal government was the most effective entity to address major problems of national concern, such as the pandemic and its impact on the economy, the infrastructure, and voting rights.

DOI: 10.4324/9781003176978-12

The new president's faith in government was consistent with his party's ideology and his personal experience of four decades of public service. It accorded with his desire to promote unity, reduce public dissatisfaction with government and its leadership, and produce a more just and equitable society. He took the preamble to the Constitution literally.[1]

A variety of empirical and subjective data supported Biden's contentions about the public's current level of dissatisfaction and distrust of government. When he took office in January 2021, only 11 percent of the people were satisfied with the way things were going in the United States, and 88 percent were dissatisfied; only a quarter of the population had a great deal or fair amount of trust in government to handle domestic and international problems; most did not. Confidence in the major institutions of the national government was low, ranging from 40 percent for the Supreme Court to 39 percent for the presidency and to 13 percent for Congress; next to the pandemic and unemployment, the government itself was perceived as the country's most important problem.[2] Seventy-eight percent of the people believed that crime was rising in the United States, even though Justice Department data showed it was not.[3] The way to build such trust was to show that government could work, that it could improve unsatisfactory conditions, and that it could generate a proud, public spirited response, echoed in the words of John F. Kennedy: "Ask not what your country can do for you—but what you can do for your country."[4]

The president planned to use the executive branch to promote his administration's policy priorities. Regulatory protections were issued in the areas of climate control, economic and social discrimination, job pay, and aid to small businesses and farmers. In mid-June, the White House issued a formal regulatory agenda for these and other policy goals.

Improving Executive Branch Operations

Boosting morale in the federal workforce was one of Biden's principal objectives, but one that he did not achieve in his first 18 months according to surveys of civil servants conducted by the Office of Personnel Management.[5] His speeches and memos to executive officials lauded the work civil servants had done; he asked agency heads to identify the problems that the previous administration had aggravated and design strategies to deal with them. Unlike Trump, who announced a hiring freeze upon taking office, Biden wanted to fill openings immediately, especially in agencies whose personnel had been greatly diminished during the Trump years. He issued an executive order to increase diversity in the civil service, presenting more job opportunities for underrepresented minorities, women, and younger people. However, the administration's hiring process was slowed by several factors: initially, agencies lacked the information to determine how many positions they had the funds to fill. Identifying experienced and technologically skilled personnel had to comport to the diversity specifications the administration adopted.[6] The absence of confirmed nominees to direct the Office of Personnel Management, Office of Management and Budget, and General Services Administration further hampered the executive branch's appointment process.

The president also asked agencies to track their performance goals, budget priorities, and improve coordination on joint agency projects, but he also instructed them not to issue any new regulations for 60 days until his administration had reviewed and modified Trump's regulatory rules and processes. Biden repealed several of his predecessor's executive orders that limited hiring and defined the cost-benefit analysis that agencies were required to use. Biden and wanted to centralize the regulatory review process.

Climate change was an important component that he wanted agencies to factor into their decision-making processes. As mentioned previously, he had revoked permits for oil and gas leases on federal lands, prevented the disposal of coal waste into streams and other bodies of waters, and built in climate improvement into his infrastructure bill and massive social legislative proposals. The president relied on the *Congressional Review Act* to reimpose methane standards.

At the end of May when the president's 2022 fiscal year budget was released, it contained funds to increase the number of civil servants by 50,000 employees. The largest increases in personnel were to be in Border Security, Labor, and Housing and Urban Affairs, followed by the Energy, Transportation, and Interior Departments, the Environment Protection Agency, and the National Science Foundation. Along with a proposed 2.7 percent salary increase, larger than any of Trump's, Biden was determined to revive and expand the federal workforce needed to govern although the freeze on salaries that exceeded $176,300 for political appointees hampered his efforts, especially to hire senior science and technology experts.[7]

Identifying qualified candidates, adhering to the merit-based hiring practices, and obtaining the necessary security clearances also slowed the hiring process. Some agencies, such as border security and the prison sys-tem, were able to increase their staff more quickly than those requiring highly educated staff, especially in the scientific and technological fields. One way the administration quickened the process was by rehiring senior civil servants who had disagreed with Trump's loyalty requirements, the authority his political appointees exercised, and the policies he was pur-suing, and left government as a result of these factors.

The opposite problem was removing Trump's political appointees who had secured civil service positions. Another was to identify women and minorities who were qualified for senior executive branch positions, especially those in the Senior Executive Service (SES). Women com-prised only about one-third of the SES and Hispanics 3 percent when Biden took over.

Partisanship was also a factor in some agencies' hiring. Republicans objected to enlarging the number of investigators in the Internal Revenue Service (IRS), alleging it was a subtle form of increased taxation. Biden had argued that about $700 billion in additional revenue could be gen-erated over the next decade by the IRS having greater capacity to inves-tigate unreported income. A report issued by the public interest group ProPublica revealed that the wealthiest Americans paid a much lower percentage of their income in taxes than did middle-class Americans.[8]

The Biden administration, learning from the pandemic, expanded telework to prevent the spread of the virus and also to save money. The executive branch had operated a top-down, risk-averse management system and had been slow to embrace teleworking. Prior to the pan-demic, only 3 percent of the daily workforce worked at home or at cen-ters outside of cities. During the pandemic, that percentage rose to 59 percent. On the basis of this experience as well as a survey conducted by the Office of Personnel Management (OPM) that revealed government workers found telework at home more satisfying than going to the office every day,[9] Biden asked agency heads to reexamine the issue of working at a remote location at home or in a regional government center. Mid-July was set as the date for this reevaluation of telework by the federal agencies. The Office of Management and Budget (OMB) and the OPM provided the guidelines for more flexible working hours, evaluating per-formance at a distance, readjusting pay differentials based on residence rather than office location, and providing equipment and supplies for telework, the principal issues that had to be resolved.[10] They did so in late July 2021; in November the OPM encouraged agencies to incorpo-rate telework in their strategic workforce plans.

Comparative Capsule 9.1   The Civil Service System

BIDEN	TRUMP
Viewed the Executive Branch favorably	Viewed most of the executive branch skeptically at best and unfavorably at worst
Wanted to enhance, enlarge, and boost morale in the civil service system	Wanted to decrease the size and operational bureaucracy of the executive branch
Increased gender and racial diversity in civil service hiring	Verified the loyalty of civil servants employed in previous administrations
Ordered as much teleworking as possible during the pandemic	Wanted federal employees to work in their offices during the pandemic

Coordinating Executive Agencies: The Role of the OMB

Within the presidency, the most important office for managing the departments and agencies is the OMB. Created by an act of Congress in 1921,
moved into the Executive Office of the President in 1939, and renamed
and reorganized to include an expanded management role in 1970, the
OMB exercises the most systemic, ongoing review of agency activities,
including their projected revenue and expenditures, policy proposals,
legislative positions, and recommendations on pending issues, testimony
before congressional committees, and issuance of regulations. The bureau
also coordinates administration policy positions with the policy councils in
the White House and the executive departments and agencies. The OMB
serves as the principal executive branch-coordinating office, clearinghouse,
and, if need be, policing authority of the presidential office.

The OMB also oversees the formulation and issuance of executive
orders and memos. It identifies the president's authority for issuing
them, costs they may generate, precedents they set, and wording of the
order itself. Executive orders are published in the *Federal Register*.

This presidential office also performs management oversight and advisory recommendations for more efficient and responsive administrative
functioning, although their management advice is less binding on agency
operations than are their budget review, legislative affairs, and regulatory review decisions. On an annual basis, the OMB evaluates the yearly
operations of the executive branch and gives departments and agencies
letter grades that could impact on their budgets, personnel, and modes
of operation.

The OMB performs these functions as a surrogate for the president
with a staff of approximately 500 civil servants and about 20 top-level

political appointees. Most presidents rely heavily on the judgment of OMB officials. They discourage department and agency heads from making special appeals to reverse OMB's decisions on budget, policy, and management issues to the president.

The principal officials of the OMB as well as the political executives of the president's policy staffs are both located in the same building, the Eisenhower Executive Office building, which is next to the White House. Communications and negotiations between the OMB and the policy staffs are ongoing, occur behind the scenes, and are resolved at the highest level necessary to determine a presidential judgment.

As former vice president, Biden was familiar with the capabilities of OMB; he announced in his first week in office that he would ask that agency to develop a revised regulatory rule-making process for the executive branch. However, after his original choice of an OMB director withdrew her nomination, he did not nominate a director to fill that position until late November.

Biden presented a summary of the government's discretionary expenditures for the 2022 fiscal year in early April and detailed his entire budget at the end of May. During much of this period, executive agencies lacked the financial data they needed to guide their review of Trump's rules and

Photo 9.1 *Office of Management and Budget Acting Director Shalanda Young testifies before the House Budget Committee*
Source: *Graeme Sloan/Sipa USA*

the cost of their implementation, revise some of the procedures and actions he established, and achieve the objectives Biden had proposed. The absence of top political appointees in confirmed positions in many of the agencies added to their difficulties and fostered a larger White House role in coordinating a response to the pandemic, immigration, and racial issues.

Confirmation Delays and Their Impact

Of the approximately 2.1 million civilian employees who work in the executive branch, about 4,000 are political appointees. The number of them requiring Senate confirmation increased by 59 percent to 1,237 since 1960.

Upon taking office, Biden appointed 1,100 people to executive branch positions, none of whom needed to be confirmed. Only 44 nominees sent to the Senate were confirmed during Biden's first 100 days; when the Senate adjourned its first session, the number reached 218; by the end of Biden's first year, the number of confirmed nominees reached 286 compared to 317 for Trump, 450 for Obama, and 505 for George W. Bush; by July 19, 2022, the total reached 400 for Biden with the rest awaiting confirmation; 89 positions had no designated nominee.[11]

In addition to the political factors he faced, the delay in determining which party would control the Senate, Trump's second impeachment trial, and the Democratic leadership's emphasis on policy rather than personnel issues, Biden also had to contend with two major institutional factors: the increasing number of political appointees and the slowing of the process for confirming them.

There are delays instituted by individual senators to halt voting on some nominees. Senator Ted Cruz (TX) held up some of Biden's foreign policy nominees because he disagreed with the administration's decision not to impose sanctions on Russia and Germany for the gas pipeline between the two countries.[12] Cruz withdrew his hold in the closing days of the first session, but only after a compromise was negotiated for a floor vote on the pipeline, a vote which Cruz lost.

Biden was also to blame for the delay in confirmed ambassadors. He did not begin to nominate them until April 2021. By mid-July, 85 ambassadorial nominations had been confirmed by the Senate, 35 more were being considered by that body while 17 ambassadorships remained unfilled. Table 9.1 lists the number of first calendar year ambassadorial nominees and confirmations by Biden and the last three of his predecessors.

TABLE 9.1   Ambassadorial Nominations and Confirmations

President	Nominations	Confirmations	Percentage Confirmed (%)
Biden	88	55	55
Trump	53	47	75
Obama	107	91	85
George W. Bush	115	103	90

Source: Partnership for Public Service's Transition Tracker

Obviously, it is difficult to recalibrate foreign policy, much less develop a new international doctrine, without the people charged with overseeing its implementation. According to Deputy Secretary of State Wendy Sherman, her meetings with Chinese officials in July would have been more informed and possibly more successful had she had the benefit of the knowledge and advice from a yet-unnominated American ambassador.[13]

Other countries' leaders were peeved as well by the slow appointment process. They resented the absence of an official U.S. ambassador; they also did not want to negotiate political matters with career officials, such as the *chargés d'affaires*, who may have had experience and knowledge but not the political contacts and clout that ambassadors usually have.

In the absence of confirmed nominees in top executive branch positions, a president has to depend on acting agency heads, some of whom may have worked in the previous administration and whose loyalty and qualifications have to be evaluated and reconfirmed.

A related problem was getting rid of Trump's political appointees, most of whom held their positions at the pleasure of the president. Biden asked Trump's personnel to resign, and most of them did. Political appointees that served fixed terms in offices were more difficult to remove, although the Supreme Court had said in 2021 that the president had the power to do so. Biden subsequently terminated the Director of the Consumer Financial Protection Agency and the head of the Federal Housing Finance Agency, which oversees the mortgage giants Fannie Mae and Freddie Mac. When he asked Andrew Saul, the head of the Social Security Commission, to resign, Saul refused to do so; the president then fired him and took his name off the Social Security website. Saul threated legal action, as did a few other members of boards appointed for a specified number of years.

Management Issues

The number of appointments, nominations, and removals, plus the large number of unfilled positions for which a nominee has not even been designated, make it difficult for the new president to "hit the ground running" and oversee the management of government. Biden suffered his first major management problem on immigration. The Secretary of Health and Human Services, who handles many of the social aspects of detention issues, had been the last department head to be confirmed, almost two months after Biden was inaugurated. The Department of Homeland Security handled most of the initial problems, but when its border guards were overwhelmed and detention facilities overcrowded and understaffed, the White House turned to other agencies to help. The fiscal years of 2021 and 2022 had the largest number of arrests and detentions of illegal immigrants on record.[14]

The administration's response to the pandemic did not suffer a similar fate, at first because the response was coordinated by a large White House staff working directly with the appropriate agencies, including the Federal Emergency Management Agency and the Department of Defense. In December 2020, Biden stated he wanted 100 million doses of the vaccines available by the end of his first 100 days. He substantially exceeded that goal. By the end of July 2021, 326 million doses had been distributed.

But it was too soon to take a victory lap. The emergence and rapid spread of the Delta variant of the virus, primarily among the unvaccinated population, but also and to a lesser extent among those who had received the vaccine, indicated that the pandemic was far from over. The administration seemed less prepared to tackle this new and more infectious variant of the virus despite the fact that other countries, such as India, England, and Israel, had experienced it and had data on its transmission and severity and on declining immunity of those who received a COVID vaccination.

When the Centers for Disease Control and Prevention (CDC) announced that the Delta virus was much more infectious than other strains, that even the vaccinated could get it and transmit it, even though their infections were not likely to be as severe or life-threatening, when Israeli studies showed that vaccine immunity decreases over time and requires booster shots, and when the number of Delta infections mushroomed in July and August, the administration did not provide a coordinated and comprehensive strategy for dealing with the spread of the pandemic. The information the public received from government health agencies was inconsistent and incomplete.

Partial administrative responses to the problem began in July when the CDC reversed its masking and social distancing requirements for vaccinated Americans and the president issued an order that workers in government facilities be vaccinated or subjected to regular COVID tests. That order became more restrictive in September when the president mandated that all federal workers and contractors be vaccinated. He also asked the Department of Labor to impose testing and vaccination rules on all companies that employed 100 or more people with penalties on single violations. Government workers and contractors had 75 days to comply or face dismissal proceedings. Public debate and legal challenges to these government requirements accelerated along partisan and ideological lines.

The third major management issue for the administration occurred in August 2021 during the withdrawal of American military forces from Afghanistan. That problem is discussed in detail in Chapter 13.

At the beginning of December, the administration announced a new management initiative designed to empower, engage, and improve the on-the-job experience for federal executives and facilitate their communication within the executive branch and with the general public. Achieving greater diversity in hiring and identifying younger candidates for federal jobs to counter the aging of the bureaucracy were also part of the Biden initiative.

The OPM is the chief human resource and personnel policy manager. It is charged with overseeing the merit-based civil service system. Trump wanted to move the office into the General Services Administration, but was unable to do so.

The President's Use of Executive Orders

The slow pace of legislation has left Biden with little alternative but to continue to issue executive orders to further the Democrats' policy agenda. In his second 100 days, most of Biden's orders pertained primarily to national security issues, such as the maintenance of national emergency declarations against countries whose governments have violated basic human rights and democratic practices: Somalia, Syria, Iraq, Yemen, North Korea, Central African Republic, Belarus, and areas such as the Western Balkans and Hong Kong.[15] He also imposed sanctions on violators of human rights in Ethiopia's civil war.

The president continued to pressure departments and agencies to revise their strategies for diversity in their hiring, reduce inequity in their decisional outcomes, take climate into account when making budgetary decisions or issuing new regulations, and depend on expert analysis and sound scientific evidence in determining their administrative judgments. In July, he issued an executive order promoting competition in the American workplace, an order directed at monopolistic practices by large companies, such as Amazon, Google, and Facebook. The first order in August pertained to electrifying cars and trucks with the imposition of new government emission standards by 2030. In September, he issued the order on expanded vaccination requirements for government workers and contractors and businesses that employed more than 100 people.

TABLE 9.2 The Exercise of Executive Authority

	Biden 2021		
Month	**Executive Orders**	**Memo Notices**	**Proclamations**
January	24	9	4
February	10	1	6
March	3	0	23
April	5	0	33
May	5	2	20
June	4	7	12
July	1	2	5
August	4	4	1
September	8	1	26
October	4	2	29
November	3	1	13
December	6	2	7
January 1–19, 2022	0	0	0
Total	**77**	**31**	**179**

President	**Other Recent Presidents in Their First Year**			**Entire Term (Number of Years)**		
Trump	55	119	570	69	220	(4)
Obama	28	128	1,227	78	276	(8)
George W. Bush	54	115	937	51	291	(8)
Clinton	57	114	652	85	364	(8)

Source: Federal Register, U.S. Government

In October, he reversed Trump's order that prohibited the government's family planning program from referring women seeking abortions to a provider of such services.

Judicial challenges to these executive actions continued. The Supreme Court ruled that the CDC did not have the authority to place a moratorium on evictions and that the government's argument for reversing Trump's "Remain in Mexico" policy for asylum seekers was not sufficient and ordered the Trump rule reinstated. Most of the vaccination mandates, however, have been upheld by lower courts but also appealed to the next judicial level. Judicial confrontations on major executive actions have continued throughout Biden's first year and promise to in future years as well. (See Chapter 7.)

Table 9.2 summarizes recent presidents use of executive power to direct executive branch decision-making in their first year in office. It also lists the number of their memos, notices, and proclamations. By July 19, 2022, Biden had issued 93 executive orders, 87 memoranda, 285 proclamations, and 55 notices.[16]

Notes

1. *We the People of the United States, in Order to form a more perfect Union, establish Justice, insure domestic Tranquility, provide for the common defence, promote the general Welfare, and secure the Blessings of Liberty to ourselves and our Posterity, do ordain and establish this Constitution for the United States of America.*

2. "Trends A–Z: Trust in Government, Satisfaction with the United States, Confidence in the Supreme Court, Presidency, and Congress, Most Important Problem," *Gallup Poll*, January, 2021; "Trust in Government: 1958–2021," *Pew Research Center*, May 17, 2021.

3. John Gramlich, "What the Data Says (and Doesn't Say) About Crime in the United States," *Pew Research Center*, November 20, 2020.

4. John F. Kennedy, Inaugural Address, 1961.

5. Erich Wagner, "Federal Employees Are Growing Less Engaged and Less Satisfied," *Government Executive,* April 28, 2022. Erich Wagner, "Federal Employee Morale is Falling," Government Executive, July 13, 2022.

6. Only 8 percent of the civil servants were under 30, compared to 23 percent in the private sector. Joe Davidson, "Biden's Proposed Budget Boosts Feds and Sidesteps Civil Service Reform for Now," *Washington Post*, June 8, 2021.

7. Eric Katz, "Agency Hiring Initiatives and Other Takeaways From Biden's First Budget," *Government Executive*, June 1, 2021; updated by Katz on April 20, 2022.

8. Paul Wiseman and Marcy Gordon, "ProPublica: Many of the Ultra-Rich Pay Next to No Income Tax," *ProPublica*, June 8, 2021.

9. "OPM Releases Government-wide Results From 2020 OPM Federal Viewpoint, Survey," *Office of Personnel Management*, April 26, 2021.

10. Lisa Rein, "Federal Telework Expected to Last," *Washington Post*, May 25, 2021; Lisa Rein and Eric Yooder, "Agencies Urged to Embrace Telework," *Washington Post*, June 11, 2021.

11. "Joe Biden Has Picked 539 Nominees to Fill Key Roles in His Administration So Far," *Partnership for Public Service*, June 15, 2022.

12. Senator Josh Hawley (MO) also held up confirmation of nominees in the foreign policy and national security arenas. He blamed top officials in the State and Defense Departments and National Security Council for the chaotic withdrawal from Afghanistan and wanted all of these officials to resign.

13. "Political Appointee Tracker," *Washington Post* and the *Partnership for Public Service*.

14. Miriam Jordan, Zolan Kanno-Youngs, and Michael D. Shear, "U.S. to Admit Up to 100,000 Refugees as Ukraine Exodus Floods Europe," *Washington Post*, March 25, 2025.

15. Memos to the Secretaries of State, Defense, and a few other agencies were also issued on the delegation of authority to implement legislation enacted by Congress for forthcoming events, such as Expo 2027 in Minnesota.

16. Ballotpedia.

CHAPTER 10

THE PRESIDENT AND THE LEGAL SYSTEM

A principal goal of the Biden administration was to revitalize the Justice Department, which the president believed that his predecessor politicized. When introducing his selection of Merrick Garland as Attorney General, Biden remarked, "More than anything, we need to restore the honor, the integrity, the independence of the Department of Justice that's been so badly damaged."[1]

That independence on nominations, positions, and policies that the Department of Justice has pursued includes questioning its decision to defend former President Trump against a defamation of character suit brought by a writer who alleged he raped her in the 1990s and not to prosecute former Trump officials, such as Secretary of Commerce Wilbur Ross, who misled Congress about the reason why his department wanted to include a question about citizenship on the census. The Supreme Court ruled against including the question.

The Biden administration was also embarrassed by the revelation that the Federal Bureau of Investigation (FBI), for investigative purposes, had been seeking subpoenas for telephone and email communications of some reporters. Once Biden announced that the practice was "very, very wrong and would not be allowed to happen again," the department announced its discontinuation. There were other issues in which Justice Department policies surprised, conflicted, or were viewed as problematic by the Biden administration.

In July 2021, the attorney general issued a memo to personnel in the department on communicating with the White House to ensure the Justice Department's independent decision-making ability. The memo desired to avoid practices in the Trump administration in which the president and his senior aides pressured the department on its investigations

Photo 10.1 *President Biden with Attorney General Garland*
Source: AP Photo/Andrew Harnik

and litigation policies. Garland also began to take a more active role in addressing crime, guns, and other public judicial issues.

The Department of Justice

The Justice Department is a multifaceted agency. It is composed of various divisions tasked with interpreting legal policy, investigating and charging violators of that policy, and defending the government against lawsuits that challenge its actions and policy judgments. The areas within the department's jurisdiction include antitrust activities, civil rights, environmental justice, governmental transparency, gun rights and restrictions, health matters and illegal drugs, human trafficking, legal policy, property rights, and tribal justice. The department also advises the president on judicial appointments; interdepartmental political appointments, including U.S. attorneys; and pardons, commutations, and reprieves. In addition to its legal staff, the department includes bureaus that investigate, enforce, and incarcerate those found guilty of federal crimes. These include the Drug Enforcement Agency, the FBI, the U.S. Marshals Service, and the Federal Bureau of Prisons.

The growing litigation of political matters has enhanced the Justice Department's role, reach, and influence. Lawsuits against the government filed by states, political parties, and individuals, businesses, and various groups have mushroomed in recent years. During and after the 2020 election, 61 lawsuits were filed in seven states by Trump's backers, challenging the results of the vote. The suits against the national government included challenges to free speech policies, prisoner and detainees' rights, and social media misinformation, and even public officials, including the president.

The Justice Department has to decide which lawsuits to prosecute and to defend. In one of its first judicial actions during Biden's presidency, the department asked the Supreme Court to drop Trump-initiated lawsuits to deny immigrants eligibility for federal benefits, drop the challenge to international medical clinics that referred patients to abortion services, and drop the lawsuit against former national security advisor John Bolton for allegedly revealing classified information in his book, criticizing Trump's foreign policy knowledge and his judgment in decision-making. The department also dropped an accompanying lawsuit against Bolton to obtain the book's profits for himself, and a lawsuit that claimed that Yale University discriminated against Asian Americans in its admissions policy.

Although the department defended the provision in *The American Rescue Plan Act of 2021* that prohibited states from using stimulus money to offset tax cuts, it also defended a defamation of character suit against Trump filed by a woman writer who accused him of rape. To defer criticism for its actions, the Justice Department was careful not to defend Trump's remarks, but only his legal status as president against such lawsuits. Democrats, however, complained that the department was too slow in reversing Trump's policies and were outraged that it was defending Trump.

The department took a strong stand on the January 6 riots, with the FBI investigating individuals who violated the law, prosecution lawyers charging violators with crimes in court, and the Justice Department refusing to immunize a member of Congress who participated in the event, arguing that the member was not performing congressional duties at the time. It also faced the problem of whether to charge Steve Bannon, an early Trump advocate and advisor, with criminal contempt after the House vote to do so and the president had said that he should be charged, a comment that the attorney general viewed as unhelpful because it jeopardized the department's independent judgment. Bannon was subsequently charged.

In the area of voting rights, Attorney General Garland announced that he was doubling the size of his department's civil rights division to examine current state laws and practices to determine whether any discriminated against non-Whites in their access and exercise of voting. A lawsuit was filed against Georgia's new election law on the grounds that it engaged in discriminatory voting practices that violated the *Voting Rights Act of 1965*. But judiciary challenges are time consuming, often appealed, and may take years to resolve.

A more contentious issue involved the FBI's subpoenaing of journalists' testimony and emails. The White House claimed that it was unaware of such actions, but the president quickly condemned them as "very, very wrong" and promised that it would not happen again in his administration. The Justice Department announced that it was ending this type of investigatory policy.

The government also challenged a new Texas law that prohibited abortions after six weeks of pregnancy and provided financial benefits for citizens to enforce the law against anyone who contributed to its violation. In its legal challenge, the Justice Department claimed that the law violated constitutionally protected rights as stated in the Fourteenth Amendment. But who to sue was another issue, since the law was to be enforced by private citizens, not the state.

One issue directly affected presidential power. Presidents have used *executive privilege* to shield internal White House discussions and papers from the public. They have done so to ensure that the president receives full and candid advice. To achieve this objective, presidents try to keep private advice they receive from being contaminated from public scrutiny.

A congressional committee investing the January 6 insurrection requested documents from the Trump White House to assess its involvement in the Capitol riot. On the advice of his legal counsel and the Department of Justice, Biden ordered the release of the information the House committee desired. Trump challenged Biden's decision and initiated litigation, claiming that executive privilege has been considered a necessary component of the presidency. Biden argued that it did not apply to ex-presidents. A federal district judge ordered the release of the documents. In her ruling, she wrote, "Presidents are not kings and Plaintiff is not President." Trump's lawyers immediately appealed the decision to the U.S. Court of Appeals. A three-judge panel put a temporary hold on the release as it considered Biden's constitutional authority to give the order, but subsequently upheld it. Trump's lawyers appealed that decision to the Supreme Court. On January 19, 2022, the Supreme Court ruled against him, upholding the Court of Appeal's decision and allowing the Archives to give the documents to the House committee.

Judicial Decisions and Their Consequences

The early judicial rulings were not favorable for the Biden administration. Federal judges reversed the president's order for a 100-day moratorium on deportations. The Supreme Court ruled in three "Shadow Docket" decisions, made over the summer when the Court was not in official session, that the administration did not demonstrate sufficient reason to reverse Trump's "Remain in Mexico" policy for immigrants seeking asylum in the United States; ruled that the Centers for Disease Control and Prevention exceeded its authority to extend the moratorium on evictions; and upheld Texas's new restrictive law that would ban all abortions at about six weeks of pregnancy with no exceptions, and allow citizens to arrest abortion violators. The president denounced that Court decision, as did most Democrats, but the Democratically controlled Congress lacked the votes to overturn it with new legislation. On June 24, the Court gave the states the power to limit or ban abortion when it reversed *Roe v Wade*.

On the other hand, the Supreme Court's ruling against the administration's reversal of Trump's "Remain in Mexico" policy for those seeking asylum in the United States gave the Biden administration more time to design a more comprehensive immigration policy without encouraging a flood of immigrants who remained in the country. It also provided leverage for the administration in dealing with progressive Democrats who wanted to increase the number of people given asylum. Only 29 percent of asylum requests were granted during the Trump presidency; by the end of the 2021 fiscal year, the Biden administration had granted 37 percent of requests.[2]

Other Judicial Issues

Biden initiated a new national security policy against domestic terrorism in June 2021 and charged the attorney general with announcing and implementing it. The new strategy was intended to reverse the emphasis on international terrorism that guided the FBI and Justice Department since 9/11 and examine internal actions that threatened democratic values and constitutional protections.

The administration also announced a major antitrust initiative aimed at companies whose size and practices impede economic competition. To jump-start this initiative, the president issued an executive order for the Department of Justice and Federal Trade Commission to closely examine mergers, employee noncompetitive agreements, and the monopolistic actions in technology and other industries in which corporate giants, such as Google, Facebook, and Amazon, exercise disproportionate influence. Biden nominated experienced lawyers to head the divisions and agencies that monitor these activities and drafted briefs to defend the president's actions.

In another legal judgment, the White House said it would not impose the death penalty on seven defendants who were sentenced in federal criminal cases.

Nomination and Confirmation of Judges

Nomination disagreements within the department paled by comparison with the lobbying over judicial appointments by Democratic senators, outside groups, and senior White House advisors. Much like Trump, Biden prioritized judicial nominations since many executive decisions that the president makes and legislation that Congress enacts are challenged by groups in the courts.

Since federal judges have lifetime appointments, they cannot be forced out by Congress, except by the impeachment process in very unusual cases. The last impeachment of a federal judge occurred in 1989. The judge, Alcee Hastings, who had been accused of perjury, tampering with evidence, and soliciting a bribe, was convicted on eight Articles of Impeachment by the Senate. Hastings later appealed his conviction and won, enabling him to run for national office. In 1993, he was elected to Congress and served until his death in 2021.

Other than removal by impeachment, other alternatives include increasing the number of Supreme Court Justices or indirectly affect their tenure by limiting their compensation and benefits or restrict their length of service. Franklin Roosevelt's attempt to "pack" the Supreme Court with more justices failed in 1937; in 2021, progressive Democrats, frustrated by the conservative orientation of the Supreme Court, suggested increasing its size. Chief Justice John Roberts had recommended more federal judges be appointed in lieu of increasing the size of the Court; the president established a commission, based in the White House, to study the matter.

The problems newly elected president's face when partisan control of the White House changes, is that they inherit a judiciary composed of a disproportionate number of judges appointed by a president of the other party, especially if that president has served two terms in office. Of the judiciary Biden inherited, one-quarter had been nominated by Trump, a large number of them at the Court of Appeals level (54) and three on the Supreme Court.[3]

Out of the 870 full-time judges, there were only 46 vacancies on the federal bench when Biden took office; federal judges tend to retire at approximately five per month. Trump began his presidency with 108 vacancies because the Republican-controlled Senate had opposed the confirmation of many of Obama's nominees in his last two years as president. Clinton had the most vacancies to fill at the beginning of his presidency, 111; George W. Bush had 84; and Barack Obama had 54.

Trump had moved quickly and successfully to fill judicial vacancies. Biden's objective was to do so as well, but with executive branch confirmations and critical legislation consuming Senate deliberations, the informal requirement of soliciting recommendations from senators of the president's party for judges who would be serving in their states, the need to vet candidates within the party, and the need to select qualified individuals that met Biden's criteria for diversity slowed initial nominations.

President Biden did not begin to nominate judges until March 2021. By July 20, 2022, he had nominated 120 judges, 74 of whom had been confirmed by the Senate with 76 vacancies still remaining in the federal court system. (See Table 10.1 for comparative data on recent presidents.)

Mitch McConnell, the Senate's Republican leader, indicated that Biden's subsequent judicial nominees were likely to meet more resistance because the president had nominated fewer judges from red states that had two GOP senators; rather, he had followed the practice of most presidents to first notify and then gain the approval from states that had two Democratic senators.[4]

Biden desired a judiciary reflective and representative of the entire country, not just major corporate law firms. He wanted judges who would meet his diversity goals and had educational, professional, and

TABLE 10.1 Comparative Judicial Confirmations of Recent Presidents (from their Inauguration to July 1 of their Second Year in Office)

	Confirmations		
President	**SC**	**CA**	**DC**
Biden	1	16	52
Trump	3	21	20
Obama	2	9	20
George W. Bush	2	9	48
Clinton	2	11	60

Note: SC, Supreme Court; CA, Courts of Appeal; DC, District Courts.

Source: Ballotpedia. (https://ballotpedia.org)

social backgrounds that had been traditionally underrepresented on the bench. He had inherited a judicial system in which two-thirds of the judges were men; 73 percent of all judges were White, 12 percent African American; 8 percent Hispanic; 4 percent Asian American; and the rest of mixed race or other.[5] Trump's confirmed judges were 84 percent White and 76 percent men.[6]

President Biden was determined to change the gender and racial balance of the federal judiciary. His nominees during the first Senate session of the 117th Congress included 75 percent women and more than two-thirds people of color who had been former public defenders, immigration, and labor attorneys.[7] The Senate confirmed Caucasan judicial candidates more quickly than those of color during this session.[8]

The Presidential Commission on the Supreme Court

In December, the Presidential Commission on the Supreme Court of the United States that Biden had established in April 2021 issued its report in a letter to the president. It examined the court's independence, its alignment with public opinion in a democratic society, its history of reform debates and proposals for change, its size, tenure of the justices, and the possibility of limiting their terms of service. No recommendations were included in its final report.

Although the public and many legal scholars support term limits for Supreme Court Justices, members of Congress of both parties have

Comparative Capsule 10.1   Major Judicial Goals

BIDEN	TRUMP
Improve the independence and integrity of the Justice Department (DOJ)	Influence DOJ's top officials and major actions to accord with the president's desires
Involve the DOJ on alleged violations of voting rights	Involve the DOJ on national security and drug issues
Rapidly nominate and confirm federal judges	Rapidly nominate and confirm federal judges
Establish commission to study the relationship between the Supreme Court and American democracy	Did not tamper with the size or operation of the Supreme Court

raised objections. Democrats believe that a constitutional amendment would take too long and probably not be ratified by enough states, while Republicans see the change as a Democratic maneuver to politicize the Court and gain seats on it.[9]

On April 26, 2022, Biden granted clemency to 78 individuals, consisting of three pardons and 75 commutations.

Notes

1. Alex Thompson, Josh Gerstein, and Theodoric Meyer, "Biden's Garland Headache," *Politico*, June 8, 2021.
2. Sandra Sanchez, "Migrants Granted Asylum at Higher Rate Under Biden Administration, New Data Shows," *Border Report*, November 15, 2021.
3. Although federal judges serve for life, they retire or assume senior status at the rate of about five per month. More leave at the beginning of a new administration that shares their political orientation.
4. Partisan politics on nominations was also fueled by Dick Durbin (IL), the chairman of the Senate's Judiciary Committee, who said he would not consider opposition from individual Republican senators but would from individual Democratic senators. Seung Min Kim and Ann E. Marimow, "Biden Moves Faster Than Trump on Court Picks," *Washington Post*, December 20, 2021.
5. "Diversity of the Federal Bench," *American Constitution Society*, August 8, 2021.
6. Ibid.
7. Ibid.
8. Tina Sfondeles, Emily Cadei, Alex Thompson, and Max Tani, "Care to Confirm," *Politico: West Wing Playbook*, December 17, 2021.
9. Seung Min Kim and Robert Barnes, "Term Limits for Justices Unlikely to Advance," *Washington Post*, December 29, 2021.

PART IV

THE PUBLIC PRESIDENCY

CHAPTER 11
BIDEN'S BULLY PULPIT

Since the beginning of the 20th century, presidents have been actively involved in the public arena. Grover Cleveland was the first president to have a press secretary; Theodore Roosevelt traveled across the country to build public support for his policy goals and personal popularity. Woodrow Wilson followed Roosevelt's example, making speeches for his domestic proposal and the League of Nations before he was felled by a massive stroke. Franklin D. Roosevelt was the first to use radio effectively in communicating with a broad section of American people. Dwight Eisenhower, followed by John Kennedy, held the first televised press conferences; Eisenhower's were filmed and then released, Kennedy's were live. The televised presidential press conference became standard fare, with the national news networks jockeying for recognition from the president.

The number of White House aides helping the president with press relations expanded. President Richard Nixon set up the first communications office in the White House in 1969; Ronald Reagan's communications director, Mike Deaver, orchestrated Reagan public appearances; Bill Clinton, with help from his vice president, Al Gore, established the first White House website; Barack Obama set up the first digital strategy operation, using files from his campaigns to reach younger supporters online. Donald Trump amplified the use of social media with his tweets and Facebook communications to gain attention, make news, and express his personal feelings, policy preferences, and evaluations of others, including the news media. The press covered Trump's social media remarks and reactions to them as standard news items.

DOI: 10.4324/9781003176978-15

The Communications Model

Biden believed that public relations is essential for the modern presidency in a democratic society. He used it to inform the public, to empathize with their needs and problems, and to build and maintain support for his programs and actions. He did not, however, regard Trump's idiosyncratic communication style, in which the president was always front and center, always making news, always appealing to his base, as appropriate or consistent with his own personal style of interacting with people. Biden's White House reverted to a more traditional presidential communications model with surrogates, not the president, meeting with the news media, organized groups, and significant others on a regular basis.

The president rarely held more than two public events a day at the beginning of his presidency; his speeches were carefully scripted to reinforce policy messages and enhance personal imagery. He held fewer one-on-one interviews than his predecessors, 22 in his first year compared to 92 for Trump. Biden avoided the print press; he preferred televised town meetings and held three on CNN during his first 8 months in office. The queries during these sessions tended to be less intrusive than those of investigatory journalists, permitting Biden to provide the answers in his own words and sound more authentic in doing so. In his third CNN town meeting in October, he detailed many of the inclusions and exclusions that were likely to appear in the *Build Back Better* bill, which Democrats were debating.

Biden established a large communications operation in the White House, consisting of offices that directed traditional and online communications and handled national and local press relations, digital strategy, speech writing and research, and scheduled meetings and events with a wide variety of groups interested in public policy. A separate office handled state and city concerns.

Of these offices, the communications unit was the largest with a staff of about 40, composed primarily of women. Kate Bedingfield, who served Vice President Biden in a similar capacity and served as deputy manager of his 2020 campaign, headed the office and participated in the meetings of senior advisors with the president. Supplementing the Communications Office were offices that handled public engagement, digital strategy outreach, and the news media. Jen Psaki, his first Press Secretary,[1] held daily press conferences, as did some of her aides who traveled with the president. The White House website provided "readouts" of

Photo 11.1 *President Biden answers a reporter's question at the last press conference of the first year in office in January 2022*
Source: AP Photo/Susan Walsh

the president's speeches, actions, and meetings, as well as fact sheets for the news media.

Although the communications staff performed traditional public relations functions, it operated very differently from Trump's. Messaging was highly disciplined and carefully coordinated. In his early months, Biden preferred others to convey the administration's position, relying primarily on his press secretary and her staff to meet with media representatives. He held very few press conferences himself; the first one occurred almost two months after he took office and the last on January 19, 2022.

Biden's public appearances increased over the course of his presidency with more events at which he spoke and more news media interviews. He also participated in several televised town halls. Table 11.1 compares the number of recent presidents' public meetings with the news media.

In addition to the press secretary and her deputies, other senior White House officials, such as the coronavirus task force, also met with the press regularly. They were accompanied by medical experts when appropriate. The press offices coordinated the appearances of cabinet officers for television and radio interviews. Secretary of Transportation Pete

Table 11.1 Presidential Press Events

Press Event	Biden	Trump	Obama	George W. Bush	Clinton
Press Conferences	19	22	27	19	38
Interviews	22	92	156	43	54
Informal Questions and Answers	216*	120	46	144	215

* Not updated by Aamer Madhani from January 9, 2021.

Source: Aamer Madhani, "Biden Shied Away From News Conferences, Interviews in Year One," *Associated Press,* January 9, 2021; updated by Madhanion January 9, 2022.

Buttigieg took the lead in promoting the infrastructure proposals with the press and public. When the legislation was enacted, however, it was the president who took the credit for his administration and the members of Congress who helped enact it. The bottom line for Biden's public relations was the imagery contrast with his predecessor. He ordered the White House to keep lines of communication open and provide details of his day, meetings, travels, speeches, and actions to national news sources and increasingly to local media. Most White House leaks were purposeful, with the anonymity of the source protected.

The President's Rhetoric

Biden and Trump could not have sounded and presented themselves more differently. Biden spoke softly; he rarely raised his voice; sometimes he used a staged whisper to create a more intimate effect with his audience, especially in small meetings. He cultivated a nice-guy image and directed his remarks to a broad cross section of Americans. Biden's speeches were not flashy or particularly eloquent. He employed considerable detail to illuminate, inform, and justify his decisions, teaching and not energizing his audience. He stuck to his script most of the time, although he did answer some press questions following his speeches even though his staff urged him not to do so. They feared gaffes and remarks that might come back to haunt him, such as when Biden announced the Taliban takeover of Afghanistan after the withdrawal of American forces was "highly unlikely." Expressing themselves in private, however, the president and also the vice president tended to use more salty language with vulgarities, which their aides enjoyed because it demonstrated deep-seated feelings and more conventional ways of expressing them in meetings with colleagues and friends.

Trump, on the other hand, spoke with a raised voice and used controversial rhetoric designed to heighten emotion. He ridiculed his critics and the news media organizations that reported their comments. He presented himself as forceful, passionate, and confident. Frequently, he would deviate from prepared remarks by reiterating themes and words that aroused his supporters, much like a preacher engaging his flock. Trump spoke mostly to his base.

The "boring" versus "bombastic" contrast was both natural and purposeful for Biden's communication strategy. Both presidents told their audiences what they wanted them to hear and remember. In smaller groups, especially with older politicians, Biden tended to be less formal. He would be reminded of personal encounters he had had, words of wisdom he had received, and interactions he had with others in the group. He was also a good listener; meetings frequently exceeded their allotted time. Extended discussion and differing opinions were encouraged.

Trump tended to be less attentive and more assertive in meetings in which he participated. As president, he often indicated his preferences early and forecast the direction he would make. Biden was a more deliberative decision maker.

Comparative Capsule 11.1 Style of Personal Public Messaging

BIDEN	TRUMP
Tended to criticize Republicans, not Democrats	Ridiculed anyone regardless of party
Used politically correct rhetoric	Often used controversial rhetoric that energized his base
Held few press interviews but responded to reporters' questions at events	Held more press interviews than Biden but responded to fewer reporters' questions at events
Depended primarily on traditional news media to reach the American public and gain attention	Depended on tweets to reach the American public and gain attention

Opinion Utilization

Poll data have been a principal component in White House communications. Both public and proprietary surveys available to the administration were used primarily to demonstrate public backing for the president's principal policy initiatives, not necessarily to inform government about the scope and intensity of opinion shifts. Favorable poll results were also employed to counter news media's tendency to focus on new and existing conflicts. Consensus tended to be newsworthy, primarily when it was unexpected. Favorable public opinion on key issues became an energizing factor that the administration used to mobilize pressure on its Congress, defend international policy decisions to which some of its allies may have objected, and improve the president and his party's standing in the eyes of the public in general and the electorate in particular.

Tweets, blogs, news media interviews, press conferences, online social communications, and public statements by administrative officials, especially the president, were the modes by which the administration tried to educate and inform, shape perceptions and evaluations, and mobilize support. They were also used to enhance the president's leverage in negotiations on policy issues and to elevate his status and standing in the eyes of the public.

As the administration progressed, building public support for the president's priorities and actions, taking credit for his accomplishments, and defending his judgments became more important communication goals. Policy trumped personality.

Press Coverage

Biden received less news media coverage during the first year of his presidency than Trump did. The normalcy of his presidency was less newsworthy than his predecessor's unconventional words and actions. He also participated in fewer one-on-one interviews with the news media and did so on traditional broadcast television networks, as well as the FOX cable news network and with national and local reporters. He was less active on social media.

The tone of his coverage was slightly more favorable than unfavorable during Biden's first three months in office. After that, it turned negative, sometimes even exceeding Trump's decline during a similar period of time.[2]

Notes

1. His second Press Secretary was Karine Jean-Pierre.

2. "At 100 Day Mark: Coverage of Biden Has Been Slightly More Negative Than Positive, Varies Greatly by Outlet Type," *Pew Research Center*, April 28, 2021; Dana Milbank, "The Media Treats Biden as Badly as — or Worse Than Trump. Here's Proof," *Washington Post*, December 3, 2021.

CHAPTER 12
PUBLIC OPINION AND PRESIDENTIAL POPULARITY

Promoting Public Relations

As the issues changed in relative importance (see Appendix), so did the thrust of the administration's messages. After six months in office, the plan was to celebrate economic recovery as unemployment fell, the stock market remained strong, and economic confidence grew. Scheduled during the summer, a slower news period with Americans on vacation, Congress usually in recess, and foreign policy not a major concern, the plan was to emphasize the president's successes in July and his pending legislative agenda plan, the *Build Back Better* bill, in August. Different groups were to be targeted about how their interests would be served and the benefits the country would receive from the $3.5 trillion package that committees in the House of Representatives were fashioning. Costs would be compensated by additional taxes on corporations and the wealthy. No one with an income of $400,000 or less would have to pay more in taxes or fees. It was to be a cost-free program to improve health care, the environment, and social equity.

The public outreach was to involve the president, vice president, their spouses, members of the cabinet, and other prominent policy experts, as well as groups promoting the new policies. During August, pro-Democrat groups outspent pro-Republican groups on television, radio, and online media advertising, directing their messages to specific proposals in the *Build Back Better* bill, while the Republicans concentrated their advertising on individual Democratic members of Congress up for reelection in 2022. They spent relatively little on policies proposed in the plan.[1]

DOI: 10.4324/9781003176978-16

The Beginning of Discontent

Although there was some bad news for the administration at the beginning of this phase of communication activities, it was not expected to divert the principal campaign. Cyberattacks, ransom demands, and internal partisan frictions received attention from the news media, but the administration was confident that the president could deal with them. He convened his cybersecurity council; threatened Russia with reprisals if its government, companies, or citizens continued their hacking of American institutions, both public and private; and warned other foreign nationals not to test U.S. resolve, especially after the breach of the Colonial Pipeline's online network that shut down the flow of fuel in the Eastern United States for several days.

A series of crises in the summer and fall of 2021 involving immigration, the spread of the Delta and Omicron variants of the COVID-19 virus, the withdrawal of American troops from Afghanistan, and the growth of inflation all affected the public's assessment of how the administration was performing. (See Box 12.1.)

Box 12.1 Problems Facing the Administration After Six Months in Office

Immigration

July 2021 marked the largest influx of immigrants in 21 years. Almost 213,000 people tried to enter the country illegally; most were deported, but about 19,000 unaccompanied minors were not. They were placed in government facilities for resettlement with families, relatives, foster parents, or social organizations. Although illegal immigration usually increases in the summer, the administration seemed unprepared for the much larger numbers; border agents were overwhelmed; shelters had to be expanded quickly, and services provided to detainees at significant cost to the government; and immigration courts were overloaded with an almost 18-month backup of pending cases for asylum.

As immigration became a more important problem for Americans, especially Republicans and people living in areas in which most recent immigrants had settled, the administration responded slowly. The Department of Homeland Security moved many of its agents to the southern border and requested funds to hire additional personnel; the Department of Health and Human Services began to subcontract necessary services at the shelters to private firms; and the administration proposed to double the number of asylum agents to relieve the backup in the courts. Then in September, an influx of thousands of Haitian refugees, mostly from South America, flooded the border. Many used their life savings to reach the United States. Even though conditions in Haiti had deteriorated in 2021 as a result of natural disasters, increasing poverty, and internal turmoil, accelerated by the assassination of the country's president, the Biden administration decided to return most of the refugees to their home country. Some with relatives in the United States were allowed to stay. The initial deportation of 8,000 Haitians sparked protests from progressive Democrats, Haitian communities in the United States, and pro-immigration groups. The Haitian government also strongly objected, and the American envoy to that country resigned in protest.[2] Biden's image as a humane and kind human being suffered as a result.

The president used Title 42 of the immigration code, established by his predecessor to prevent entry and to deport illegal immigrants on the basis of COVID and other health concerns. The use of this rule prevented immigrants from seeking asylum because they were not even allowed to enter the United States. It was not until November that the deportation rules were modified to focus deportation on recent illegal immigrants who posed threats to public safety and national security, but Title 42 remained on the books and continued to be used by border security agents. The president subsequently announced that he would order an end to the use of Title 42 to curb illegal immigration, but a federal judge enjoined his order three days before the title was set to expire.

In all, 1.7 million immigrants were detained or deported in 2021, a record number for the decade. On June 13, 2022, the Supreme Court ruled that illegal immigrants can be detained indefinitely and are not entitled to a bond hearing.

Immigration continued to be a confusing and disappointing process for asylum seekers. It also generated political controversy. Republicans and moderate Democrats wanted stricter enforcement of the Migrant Protection Protocols (MPP), the "Remain in Mexico" policy, until the immigration courts made decisions on the individual applicants. Human rights advocates, including most progressive Democrats, opposed the policy on the grounds of the poor living conditions and increased criminality in the camps and the large backup of cases, about 400,000. The Biden administration explored the establishment of European-like centers for immigrants but did not do so during the president's first year.

President Biden initially suspended the MPP but was prevented from doing so by a legal decision based on a Texas and Mississippi lawsuit. That decision was later affirmed by the U.S. Supreme Court. In December 2021, the president asked Mexico to renew the agreement to require immigrants seeking asylum to remain in that country until their cases were processed, which could take years. Mexico agreed to do so. Later the Biden administration decided to end the MPP policy but was initially prevented from doing so by legal challenges. At the end of its 2021–2022 term, however, the Supreme Court ruled that the president had the authority to do so.

Another problem was how to treat families in which children were separated from their parents during the Trump administration. Progressive Democrats and pro-immigration groups proposed substantial monetary compensation that moderate Democrats and Republicans opposed. These differences were evident within the White House as well. Biden initially sided with the moderates. There has been a decline in the public's evaluation of the administration's immigration policies and actions.

The New COVID Variants

The rapid spread of the Delta and Omicron variants of the COVID virus in the summer was another critical issue that beset the country, divided the populace, renewed the vaccination and mask-wearing debates, particularly as schools were getting underway, and negatively affected the economy. Optimism turned to pessimism by the summer as the Delta and Omicron variants of the virus spread rapidly across the country.

Cases of COVID-19 increased as did hospitalizations and deaths. Although unvaccinated individuals were more likely to get seriously ill from the Delta variant of the virus, the Centers for Disease Control and Prevention also indicated that people who were vaccinated could get and spread the virus, although they were less likely to require hospitalization. That warning, illustrated by reports of vaccinated members of Congress, their staffs, and other prominent

individuals being re-infected, generated fear and changed perceptions that the pandemic was not under control, that social distancing and economic disruptions would continue into the foreseeable
future, and that the administration's information on the COVID
virus was incomplete, inconsistent, and confusing.

The confusion was also generated by the need for booster shots.
The president had indicated that they would be available at the end
of September. Scientific studies in Israel and England indicated that
the immunity provided by COVID vaccines declined over time.
But initially, U.S. government health agencies could not agree on
whether, to whom, and when to make such shots available, claiming that they needed more data to make such a judgment. The
president who had said he would follow the advice of scientists, not
politicians, was caught in a bind between those who wanted additional protection, those who were uncertain whether boosters were
necessary, and those opposed to vaccinations.

Finally, on September 24, 2021, the Food and Drug Administration (FDA) issued its first booster decision, approving the Pfizer vaccine booster for people with immune deficiencies, people 65 years of
age and older, and others in high-risk jobs six months after their last
vaccination. Biden received his booster shot three days later.

Yet the Delta and Omicron variants remained, despite the fact
that a majority of the population, about 60 percent, was fully vaccinated by the end of the summer and approved of the mask mandate,
but the public's evaluation of government health agencies declined
because of the confusing and inconsistent information they provided. The public's positive perception of the administration's pandemic strategy also lessened.[3]

In September 2021, the president responded to pressure from
the pro-vaccination constituency, mostly Democrats and Independents, who wanted to return to normalcy, to work, dine, travel,
and attend events without fear of being infected by those who were
unvaccinated, refused to wear masks, or refused to socially distance
themselves from others. He issued an executive order that required
that all federal workers and contractors, staff at facilities funded
by the government (including the Head Start program, the Defense
Department, and Native American schools), and health-care workers at institutions that accepted Medicare and Medicaid for vaccination payments be vaccinated within 75 days or regularly tested for

COVID. There were exceptions for religious beliefs or medical conditions. Republicans strongly objected to the vaccination mandate requirements, while Democrats and Independents supported them.

In addition, the president asked the Department of Labor to issue a directive that required all businesses that employed 100 or more workers and all health-care workers at hospitals that received Medicare payments be vaccinated or undergo weekly COVID testing. They had to do so by mid-January 2022, but the Labor Department later extended the date to mid-February. Substantial fines were to be imposed on private firms and hospitals that received federal funds for each violation. The new policy was estimated to affect about two-thirds of the U.S. workforce, but it was quickly challenged by opponents in almost half the states, many of which had enacted mandates against required masking and vaccination rules.

More than half of the states' attorneys general and coalitions of business and other interest groups initiated legal challenges opposing the regulation. On November 12, 2021, a three-judge Court of Appeals panel in the Fifth Circuit enjoined the enforcement on the grounds that the office in the Department of Justice, the Occupational Safety and Health Administration, lacked the authority to issue new mandate rules, but another three-judge panel in the Sixth Circuit in mid-December reversed the Fifth Circuit court decision. In early January 2022, the Supreme Court blocked the mandate on private companies but allowed it for health-care workers at hospitals that accepted Medicare and Medicaid.[4]

Following the FDA's approval of vaccinating children five years of age and older, the administration made more vaccines available and stepped up its efforts to convince parents that the vaccine was safe and would help reduce the spread of the Delta and Omicron variants among young children.

Conflicts between proponents and opponents of vaccination and mask wearing accelerated over the summer and fall.[5] States with the lowest rates of vaccinations, mostly red ones, had higher rates of infection, but the conservative Republican governors of many of those states refused to issue mask mandates, and in some cases, threatened localities and school systems that did so with financial penalties. Much litigation followed. The courts, however, were sympathetic to vaccine requirements as schools reopened and people who had been teleworking returned to their places of employment.

When the Omicron virus reached the United States, the president extended restrictions, increased the testing protocol for international travelers desiring to enter or reenter the country, banning flights from several countries in the southern part of Africa and increasing testing for international travelers entering the United States. He did not propose a lockdown or shutdown, however. Biden also announced that additional COVID testing sites would be available, and free kits for home testing would be provided by the government, but they were not distributed until January 2022. He also ordered federal agencies to increase teleworking for their employees as much as their operations permitted.

Biden continued to urge Americans to get vaccinated and receive a booster shot, which was not mandated, as their "patriotic duty." He also deployed military health-care personnel and National Guard personnel to hospitals overwhelmed with infected patients. By the end of Biden's first year, 67.9 million people in the United States had been infected with COVID-19 and 853,200 had died; by mid-July 2022, that number had increased to 90 million infected and over 1 million deaths.[6]

Immigration, COVID-19 variants, and the president's decision to withdraw American military forces from Afghanistan took much of the luster off the administration's first six months in office. During this period, the economy was recovering, the pandemic was declining, and no major foreign policy crisis was occurring. Nonetheless, Biden was blamed for the continuing pandemic and economic problems, especially inflation, problems that began in the summer of 2021. The president had promised to treat immigrants, especially children, more humanely and to increase the number of refugees let into the United States. On July 4, 2021, he announced, "We've gained the upper hand against this virus. We can live our lives. Our kids can go back to school, our economy is roaring back."[7] When he announced the withdrawal of American military from Afghanistan in July, he said, "The Taliban overrunning everything and owning the whole country is highly unlikely."[8]

Six congressional committees conducted hearings on the Afghanistan intelligence and withdrawal. Allied countries were peeved by their lack of consultation on the issue. Biden was also criticized by the American public for his slow reaction to these problems, his administration's lack of preparation for them, and for the timing of announcements.

The Economy

The economic recovery did not occur as quickly as hoped. It was once again growing, but at a slower pace than before the pandemic. Almost five million new jobs were created and unemployment declined, but many of the jobs remained unfilled. Wages increased but so did inflation, canceling out wage gains for many workers. The price increases were driven by demand, labor shortages, and disrupted supply chains, with fossil fuel energy, cars, and food all increasing in price. Republicans referred to the increase in prices as an "inflation tax."

The spread of COVID-19 variants slowed economic growth, decreased consumer confidence, and reduced support for the president's handling of the economy. Although consumer spending increased, particularly in the winter as the holidays approached, by the end of his first year, in December, 78 percent of Americans evaluated current economic conditions as fair or poor, while 70 percent indicated that their economic outlook had worsened.[9]

The administration's initial response to growing economic pessimism was to point to job growth that would be additionally spurred by the bipartisan infrastructure bill. Biden also tried to repair the disrupted supply chain by opening ports 24/7, first in southern California and then on the East Coast, increasing storage space for ship cargos, and encouraging more trucking of products. The president acknowledged the price increases, empathized with workers, and suggested that the growth in inflation would only be temporary, but Biden's words and actions alone did not reverse the spike in prices any more than they stopped the pandemic.

By the end of September 2021, a majority of Americans evidenced disapproval of Biden's presidency. His handling of the pandemic, economy, immigration, and foreign policy tarnished his personal attributes and leadership image. Fewer people saw President Biden as empathetic, principled, and a good role model. His judgment and competency were questioned. After Afghanistan, conservative criticism became louder as crowds that opposed Biden shouted, "Let's go Brandon," a version of a vulgar four-syllable word directed at the president.[10]

Although the decline of support mirrored partisan divisions, it was evident among all partisan groups. Some Republicans even questioned the president's mental agility at the age of 78 years.[11] In a poll taken in November 2021, half the public did not view him in good health.[12] News commentators highlighted the "groupthink" mentality of his senior advisors on such issues as Afghanistan and inflation. And Americans were paying more attention to the news than usual in a nonelection year.[13]

Declines in public approval of presidents are not unusual during their first year in office. (See Table 12.1.) Although the White House was concerned, the president's senior advisors hoped that the negative reaction would dissipate by the time the campaign for midterm elections began, that the economic downturn would be temporary, that the number of COVID infections would decrease, and that the economy would rebound. _____

TABLE 12.1 Presidential Job Approval (in percent)

| Month/Time Frame | Biden | | Other Presidents' Approval in Corresponding Month | | | |
	Approve	Disapprove	Trump	Obama	George W. Bush	Clinton
January 1/21–2/2, 2021	54	42	45	67	—	—
February 2/3–18	57	37	41	65	57	51
March 3/1–15	56	40	42	62	63	53
April 1–21 End of First 100 Days	54	42	40	61	59	55
May 3–18	57	40	42	66	53	45
June 1–18	51	40	37	62	55	37
July 6–21	49	42	38	58	57	45
August 2–17	43	45	36	56	55	44
September 1–17	42	48	37	52	51	47
October 1–19	42	53	38	54	87*	50
November 1–16	43	52	—	52	87	—
December 1–16	43	51	36	49	86	52
January 1–19, 2022	42	54	37	51	84	47
February 1–17	41	54	37	57	81	49
March 1–3	42	54	49	—	82	42
April 1–19	41	56	43	47	76	55
May 2–22	41	54	42	50	77	51
June 1-20	41	57	42	46	73	46

*Reflects opinion after terrorist attack on September 11, 2001.

Source: "Topics A–Z: Presidential Job Approval Ratings," Gallup Poll, 2021–2022

A New Communications Offensive

In light of these adverse events, the president canceled a planned summer vacation and returned to Washington. He met regularly with policy officials who advised him on these issues and would be responsible for implementing the administration's responses. As the sounds from the president's bully pulpit became more muted, the president's public schedule changed as well. In July 2021, Biden began an empathy campaign. Focusing on the concerns of people who had suffered from natural disasters and the Afghanistan turmoil, the president and his wife met with the families of the soldiers killed in the suicide bombing. He also reached out to those who had suffered from natural disasters on September 11, 2001, about one-third of the country.[14] He proposed that Congress enact $30 billion of additional disaster relief for them and also more money to resettle Afghans in the United States. The president visited Louisiana, New York, and New Jersey, all devastated by Hurricane Ida. On the 20th anniversary of the 9/11 terrorist attacks, he and the First Lady paid their respects to families who lost loved ones at the three sites of the plane crashes. The vice president and her spouse also

Photo 12.1 *President Biden, Vice President Harris, and their respective spouses commemorate the 20th anniversary of the September 11 terrorist attacks at a wreath ceremony at the Pentagon*
Source: *AP Photo/Alex Brandon*

went to the Pennsylvania crash site and later joined the president and military officials at a ceremony at the Pentagon.

Caring had replaced celebration, delaying but not canceling the campaign to boost support for the Democrats' human infrastructure proposals. However, the rise in inflation put the scope and cost of this program in doubt. Toward the beginning of October, that campaign was resumed.

After the president returned to the United States from his trip abroad in November, attending two climate summits, the White House began a new public relations campaign, emphasizing the importance of vaccinations and providing additional aid to the communities hardest hit by the virus, especially rural areas. Biden trumpeted the enactment of the bipartisan infrastructure bill and the job-related benefits it would provide, the climate initiatives it contained, and the improvements to the infrastructure that would make transportation faster and safer.

The president also became more critical of Republicans who opposed his legislative polices, his vaccination mandates, and purposely slowed consideration of needed legislation, such as funding the government, raising the debt limit, and delaying the enactment of the *National Defense Authorization Act for Fiscal Year 2022*, muting his quest for bipartisanship cooperation. On January 6, 2022, the one-year anniversary of the Capitol insurrection, he targeted his predecessor without ever mentioning his name, along with Republicans who defended the contestation of the election and the insurrection. Within the context of defending and applauding America's democratic values and practices, the president said:

> The former president of the United States of America has created and spread a web of lies about the 2020 election. He's done so because he values power over principle, because he sees his own interests as more important than his country's interests and America's interests, and because his bruised ego matters more to him than our democracy or our Constitution.
>
> He can't accept he lost, even though that's what 93 United States senators, his own Attorney General, his own Vice President, governors and state officials in every battleground state have all said: He lost.
>
> That's what 81 million of you did as you voted for a new way forward.

He has done what no president in American history—the history of this country—has ever, ever done: He refused to accept the results of an election and the will of the American people.

While some courageous men and women in the Republican Party are standing against it, trying to uphold the principles of that party, too many others are transforming that party into something else. They seem no longer to want to be the party—the party of Lincoln, Eisenhower, Reagan, the Bushes.[15]

The administration's national public outreach campaign emphasized legislative achievements, the economic recovery, and the benefits of the *Build Back Better* legislation pending in the House, and the threat to American democracy posed by Trump's actions and most Republicans. It involved the president, vice president, several cabinet secretaries, and pro-Democratic groups. Biden's January 6, 2022 address was designed to help the Democrats' messaging in the year of the midterm elections. Losing control of one or both houses would seriously limit the president's ability to extend his policy agenda.

President and Party Tensions

The White House had been concerned with partisan politics from the outset. The president's senior aides had replaced top personnel in the Democratic National Committee (DNC) during the transition, tasking one of the deputy chiefs of staff, Jen O'Malley Dillon, with maintaining ongoing relations with the DNC and other party committees, with the White House senior advisor, Mike Dillon, monitoring public and congressional support. Anita Dunn, a senior advisor who left the White House to return to the private sector in mid-August 2021, continued to advise the president and party officials on strategy and tactics for the 2022 midterm elections.

Tensions developed within the DNC over the party's voter data. The head of the organization wanted it to remain with the DNC, while others, including the White House, wanted it to go to an organization outside the party's national headquarters. There were also differences over the nomination of party delegates and the amount of money given to certain state parties.

Major fundraising operations were also underway, but many Democratic donors and bundlers were not happy with Biden; few had received ambassadorial appointments or much attention from the White House. Most big liberal donors wanted Biden to focus more on climate change and national voting rights.

President Biden did not play a major role in fundraising in 2021. Unlike his predecessors, he did not set up a committee to build a war chest for his reelection, and he did not participate in many fundraising events. Nonetheless, Democratic committees raised almost as much money as Republican ones in the pre-midterm election year, according to the Federal Election Commission.[16] Biden did attend fundraisers for Democrats in 2022.

Although partisan leanings remained relatively steady throughout most of 2021, several features of the electorate made the forthcoming midterm elections a major focus, affecting Democratic and Republican congressional agendas and their members' voting behavior in 2021. These included the near equal division of party identifiers, the growing number of Independents, and anticipated disadvantages that gerrymandering would produce after the 2020 census, along with new restrictive state voting laws and a few pivotal elections that could decide which party controlled the House and the Senate in 2023. Personal and ideological divisions between and within the parties did, too.[17]

The Democrats were concerned about the decline of Hispanic support in 2020, especially among Latino men, who tended to be more conservative than Latina women, and more fearful that the party's politics would lead the country in a socialist direction. From the outset, the White House and Democratic activists were determined to reach out directly to the Latino community rather than depend on Latin advocacy groups to do so. The president and First Lady held multiple meetings and telephone calls with Hispanic leaders. Ads were aired on Spanish television networks Telemundo and Univision. Dr. Jill Biden, whose first chief of staff was Latina, was particularly active in communicating with Latino groups; she even appeared on a special version of *Sesame Street* designed to appeal to children from Hispanic families. Other presidential aides, many of whom were of Hispanic ancestry, maintained their contacts with the Latin groups that proposed them for jobs in the administration, reporting on their needs and concerns to policy makers and administrators and advocating for their interests.

The White House concentrated on matters affecting the Hispanic community: health-care matters, particularly the pandemic and the need to get vaccinated; ongoing immigration issues that affected these communities; and presidential policies of particular benefit to Latino families, including childcare, minimum wage legislation, and educational proposals and opportunities.[18] Cedric Richmond, the first Director of the Office of Public Engagement in the White House, emphasized the funding that would be made available to cities and states in the *Build Back Better* plan to end the cycle of violence and increasing homicides in some racial and ethnic communities. Concern with crime and safety continued to be a major issue for voters.

The abortion issue, which reemerged by the enactment of stricter state laws that severely shortened the period in which women could obtain abortions, the leaked Supreme Court opinion by Justice Samuel Alito and later the decision itself overturning Roe v. Wade was a critical issue Democrats emphasized in their quest to enlarge and solidify their suburban vote, not only from women but also from men sympathetic to women's right to choose. Obviously, constraints on abortion were not promoted among religious Catholic or Evangelical Protestants. Democratic proposals to expand health-care coverage were also an issue that appealed to the party's base.

Democrats seeking reelection not only emphasized their party's accomplishments but also admonished Republicans who opposed Trump's impeachment, opposed the bipartisan compromise on infrastructure, opposed the protection of voting rights, and opposed masking and social distancing measures to deal with the pandemic. Those aligned with Trump in competitive congressional districts were particularly targeted, but the Democratic Party's losses in the Virginia elections of 2021 in which Trump was a major target suggested a more positive, upbeat message was needed. In his first year with so few elections, Biden did not do much campaigning on behalf of Democratic candidates.

Variations in Presidential Popularity

In addition to promoting its achievements and pledging to continue the progress made on policies, the administration's public relations campaigns also sought to elevate Biden's stature in the eyes of the public. For the first six months, his job approval ratings remained in the low- to mid-50 percent range. Democrats gave him overwhelming support and a majority of Independents viewed him favorably, but most Republicans did not, with the exception of his initial policies to combat COVID-19.

The enactment of the bipartisan infrastructure bill and a decline in unemployment growth gave the White House hope that the president's job ratings could return to his first-six-month levels. Although the public favored his new policies, those policies did not improve Biden's job approval ratings. His job approval numbers dropped by more than 10 percent, beginning in July and his popularity continued to fall. The president's handling of the pandemic, his vaccination mandates, his management of the economy, especially the spike in inflation, and the chaotic withdrawal from Afghanistan affected the public's evaluation much more than did the favorable view of his new policies. Disarray among Democrats in Congress also tarnished his and the party's images and increased the likelihood that the Democrats would lose control of one or both Houses of Congress in the 2022 midterm elections. (See Tables 12.1 and 12.2 for the variations of presidential job approval.)

Issue approval showed more variance. The public's evaluation of the president's personal characteristics remained fairly stable. Satisfaction with the direction of the country varied with the pandemic, the economy, and other conditions that affected large groups of citizens. Nonetheless, Biden did better than Trump in his first year on most issues. (See Table 12.3.)

TABLE 12.2 Biden's Job Approval by Partisanship (in percent)

Month	Democrats	Independents	Republicans
January 2021	98	61	11
February	96	53	12
March	94	50	8
April	94	58	11
May	92	54	8
June	95	55	11
July	90	48	12
August	93	43	7
September	90	37	6
October	92	34	4
November	90	37	6
December	78	40	5
January 2022	82	33	5
February	79	35	7
March	89	38	5
April	84	35	5
May	82	39	3
June	85	36	3

Source: "Topics A–Z: Presidential Job Approval Ratings," Gallup Poll, 2021–2022

TABLE 12.3 Biden's and Trump's Issue Approval

	Biden				Trump		
Month	Approve	Disapprove	No Opinion	Month	Approve	Disapprove	No Opinion
With the way the president is handling:							
The Economy							
November	36	61	1	November	45	51	4
August	46	54	1	June	45	53	2
Foreign Affairs							
November	38	59	3	November	31	61	5
August	46	51	3	June	35	62	3
February	56	40	4	February	38	57	4
Response to COVID-19							
November	49	49	2	October	40	59	1
August	51	48	1	June	42	58	1
February	67	31	2	March	60	38	1
Immigration							
November	31	66	3	October	46	52	2
September	38	60	2	September	48	52	2
August	41	57	2	June	40	59	2
				February	42	57	1
Race Relations							
August	45	52	3	August	34	64	2
				February	38	59	1

Source: "Topics A–Z: Issue Approval," *Gallup Poll*, 2021–2022

In 2022, Biden's approval ratings dropped on his handling of the economy but improved on his response to the situation with Russia after its invasion of Ukraine.

The White House followed opinion polls very carefully and used them, when they were favorable, to build and maintain public support and to pressure members of Congress to vote for issues that the public supported. These polls reported public perceptions of the most important problems as well as opinion on a range of policy initiatives. (See Appendix.)

Electioneering

With congressional elections occurring every two years and the presidential election every four, getting reelected is not far from politicians' minds. It affects their behavior in office, their public remarks, political messaging, policy positions, and actions. For the president, contemporary politics affects presidential travels, proclamations designed to recognize and praise specific groups, as well as compromises within and between the parties on major issues, all of which create a record of accomplishments on which to campaign, and of course, fundraise.

During Biden's first six months in office, he did only limited travel with most of it directed at support for his executive and legislative priorities, focusing on the pandemic and the economy. In the next six months, he traveled a lot more outside the Washington metropolitan area, excluding his regular weekend visits to his home in Delaware or Camp David. By the end of his year, he had gone to 26 states, making the most trips to the battleground states of Pennsylvania, Michigan, and Georgia. He accelerated his travel outside of Washington in the first 8 months of 2022.

The president's first trip outside the United States occurred in mid-June 2021 when Biden attended the G7 summit in the United Kingdom, a NATO conference in Belgium, and a one-on-one meeting with Russian president Vladimir Putin in Geneva. The last international trip he made during his first 18 months was to the Middle East.

Notes

1. Jonathan Lemire, "Pro-Biden Groups to Spend $100 Million on August Ad Blitz," *Associated Press*, August 2, 2021.
2. A news media story and photograph of border agents on horses using their reins to prevent Haitians from crossing the border further inflamed the situation.
3. Jeffrey M. Jones, "Americans' Ratings of CDC Communications Turn Negative," *Gallup Poll*, September 7, 2021.
4. *Biden v. Missouri* (2022).
5. Jeffrey M. Jones, "Two-Thirds in U.S. Now Say COVID-19 Situation Worsening," *Gallup Poll*, September 1, 2021.
6. "COVID Data Tracker, Centers for Disease Control and Prevention," accessed July 20, 2022.
7. Joe Biden, "Remarks by Joe Biden Celebrating Independence Day and Independence From COVID-19," *White House*, July 4, 2021.
8. Joe Biden, "Remarks by President Biden on the Drawdown of U.S. Forces in Afghanistan," *White House*, July 8, 2021.
9. "Trends A–Z: Economy," *Gallup Poll*.
10. In a Christmas telephone call to military personnel, the caller said, "Let's go, Brandon." He did not know that Biden was also on the call. The president then repeated the line in jest. Some of the president's aides were horrified that he used that expression.

11. "Biden Loses Ground with the Public on Issues, Personal Traits and Job Approval," *Pew Research Center*, September 23, 2021.

12. Marc Caputo, "Poll: Voters Split on Biden's Mental Fitness as Job Approval Remains Low," *Politico*, November 17, 2021.

13. Lydia Saad, "Political News Receives Heightened Public Attention," *Gallup Poll*, November 16, 2021.

14. Sarah Kaplan and Andrew Ba Tran, "Nearly 1 in 3 Americans Experienced a Weather Disaster This Summer," *Washington Post*, September 4, 2021.

15. "Remarks by President Biden to Mark One Year Since the January 6th Deadly Assault on the U.S. Capitol," *White House*, January 6, 2022.

16. "Campaign Finance Data," *Federal Election Commission*, January 1–December 31, 2021.

17. "Beyond Red vs. Blue: The Political Typology," *Pew Research Center*, November 9, 2021.

18. Tina Sfondeles and Alex Thompson, "West Wing Playbook," *Politico*, August 3, 2021.

PART V

THE EVOLVING BIDEN PRESIDENCY

CHAPTER 13
SUCCESSES, FAILURES, AND ONGOING FOREIGN POLICY CONCERNS

At the outset of his presidency, Biden focused on the domestic policy issues that dominated public concern, immigration being the exception. He outlined his priorities in foreign affairs: repairing European and other democratic alliances, confronting Russian internet intrusions, and China's economic and territorial expansions. He was also forced to deal with the international consequences of the global pandemic and climate change as well as myriad unexpected events that threatened democratic values, harsh autocratic policies that silenced and punished dissent, coups against elected governments, and outbreaks of fighting between Hamas and Israel. That conflict forced the president to engage in negotiations and pressure to end the hostilities. Biden's strong support for the sovereignty of Israel, its close ties to the United States, and its status as a democratic Jewish state within the context of an authoritarian, distrustful, and often hostile Arab environment required Biden to apply increasing private and public pressure on the government of Israel to accept a cessation of military activities. Domestic political divisions within Israel and within the United States complicated Biden's peacemaking initiative.

The other initial component of Biden's formulation and implementation of foreign policy was to restore the State Department's previous advisory and management responsibilities that Democrats believed had been diminished and politicized by the Trump administration. Giving career department officials more responsibility, filling vacant positions, and enhancing the department's role in policymaking were Biden's principal administrative objectives. Secretary of State Antony Blinken became the administration's primary spokesman, meeting with international leaders, coordinating common interests of allies, and testifying before Congress to explain administration actions and defend the president's policy.

DOI: 10.4324/9781003176978-18

The president also wanted an active national security advisory council with which he met frequently. The head of the council, chief advisor to the president Jake Sullivan, also became a spokesman, meeting with foreign leaders in the early months of the administration to explain the new goals and policy initiatives that the Biden administration wished to articulate, reduce and repair tensions that had built up during the Trump presidency, and seek more cooperative ways in which democracies could work together to further their mutual values and interest and counter threats from autocratic leaders who desired to expand their economic and national security within the international community.

Despite the new priorities and renewed emphasis on diplomacy, the president did not make his first major ambassadorial appointments until the end of June, although career foreign service officers were nominated for ambassadorships to smaller countries in the developing world. Biden wanted to deemphasize the practice of nominating major campaign contributors and bundlers to the prestigious U.S. embassies in Europe and Asia.

The President's Personal Diplomacy

Conversations and Meetings With Foreign Leaders

Upon taking office, Biden received the usual congratulatory calls from foreign leaders, with neighbors from Mexico and Canada being first. The calls with both country's leaders assured them of U.S. support and friendly relations, although he also indicated to Canadian Prime Minister Justin Trudeau that he would rescind the permit for the Keystone Pipeline. Western European allies received much the same good news. "America was Back"; it would rejoin the Paris Climate Accords that Trump pulled out of, and it would continue to exercise leadership within the democratic world but do so in a more cooperative manner than his predecessor. He renewed America's support for NATO, attended the G7 conference on economic matters, and rejoined and considered participating in the nuclear agreement that the European Union and the Obama administration hammered out with Iran.

Perceptions of American international leadership had declined during the Trump presidency. Americans believed that their country's reputation was important and would improve under Biden's leadership. They concurred with his emphasis on diplomacy, democracy, and cooperative international leadership.[1] These views were shared by most of America's traditional allies in Europe, Asia, and North America who strongly objected to Trump's "America First" policies and go-it-alone attitude, both of which Biden promised not to pursue. In light of decisions and actions that furthered American interests, such as its withdrawal of military forces from Afghanistan, the distinction between Trump's "America First" policy and Biden's cooperative diplomacy became more muddled.

Nonetheless, the reputation of the United States has improved under Biden's leadership. A global survey conducted by the Gallup organization six months after President Biden took office found that 49 percent of the people surveyed in 46 countries approved of U.S. leadership; 36 percent disapproved. The ratings of the Biden administration are similar to Obama's, but considerably higher than Trump's.[2]

Americans and most foreign policy leaders also expressed more confidence in Biden's personal style: his cautious and consistent decision-making and his emphasis on human rights, democratic values, and cooperative diplomacy. Biden's evaluation on these personal attributes varied between partisan lines in the United States, as well as between democratic/ antidemocratic nation states abroad.

To countries that were less friendly to the United States, particularly those challenging America's international leadership, Biden was firm and resolute. Favoring diplomacy over military confrontation, he informed adversaries of the lines that could not be crossed without invoking a serious and forceful U.S. response. Biden believed the principal role of the military was to defend the country's national security in the face of threats to its sovereignty and democratic values.

Biden's International Trips

The first international trip that President Biden took occurred in mid-June to the United Kingdom, Belgium, and Switzerland. Biden met with U.K. British Prime Minister Boris Johnson to demonstrate the continuing close alliance between the two countries. They signed a revised Atlantic Charter that reiterated their democratic values and addressed support for NATO, improvement of the environment, and opposition to cyberattacks, international hacking, and external interference in elections. The president also pledged that the United States would donate 500 million vaccines to poorer countries to combat the coronavirus; G7 countries also promised another 500 million, well short of the amount of vaccines needed to immunize the large population in less-developed countries.

The G7 meetings also discussed trade with China, on which there was not unanimity. European countries wanted the United States to eliminate or reduce Trump's tariffs on imported aluminum and steel; the United States wanted to limit Europe's economic trade with China, especially on technological contracts, such as broadband installation by Huawei, a Chinese-owned company.

The NATO meeting in Belgium was the next conference Biden attended. In addition to reiterating support for a strong NATO military alliance, the president and other NATO leaders raised concerns about China's growing military challenges, although they still saw Russian activities as their primary threat. Climate change was also acknowledged as a concern that had to be addressed.

The next day, Biden met with leaders of the European Union. The principal topic was trade. In addition to agreeing to lower tariffs, the European Union and the United States resolved the contentious issue of subsidies for major airplane manufacturers, such as Airbus and Boeing.

The final stop on Biden's European travel was to Geneva to meet with Russian President Putin. His foreign policy experts discussed Putin's responses to U.S. criticism of its election interference in 2016, cyber-attacks and ransomware directed from Russia, that country's increasing ties with China, military threats to Ukraine, and its government's harsh treatment of dissenters, including the jailing of Alexei Navalny, a political rival of Putin. Biden said he wanted Putin to "know what I want him to know." He told the Russian president that the United States would respond to Russian activities that threatened its security, such as cyberattacks, ransomware threats, and election interference, in all of which Putin had denied Russian involvement. Both leaders stood their ground, although they agreed to set up working groups to mitigate their differences, promote strategic stability, and prevent further nuclear proliferation.

The meeting enabled Biden to differentiate his attitude and approach to Russian–American relations from Trump's, to illustrate his knowledge and experience in dealing with adversaries, and to demonstrate strong leadership in a manner that was candid and consultative but not confrontational. He drew red lines, boundaries that could not be crossed, but he was careful to do so in a nonthreatening way. He urged fair competition that would not tip over to armed conflict. From the White House's perspective, the meetings with allies and with Putin enhanced Biden's stature at home and abroad. He encountered little criticism.

The trip reinforced Biden's international objectives: improving relations with allies and resisting policies by adversaries that threatened U.S. interests and security. The statements, promises, and pledge of cooperative leadership initially worked to improve American's standing in the eyes of its traditional allies. That image, however, remained tarnished by Biden's continuation of many of Trump's tariffs, travel restrictions, and withdrawal of U.S. military forces from civil strife in the Middle East.

In September, Biden tried to improve America's image by stressing climate control and pandemic relief in an address before the United Nations. He promised to purchase an additional 500 million Pfizer vaccines within the year (in addition to the 500 million in 2021) to distribute to less-developed countries with a goal of immunizing 70 percent of the world's population from the COVID virus within one year. Reaching that goal, however, also required other advanced countries to contribute millions of doses as well. Following his UN speech, Biden held a virtual summit on climate change in which he urged countries to make additional commitments to decrease fossil fuel consumption. He announced the United States would cut its own carbon emissions by one-half within the next decade, a date that seemed overly optimistic.

In November, he met with Canadian Prime Minister Trudeau and Mexican President Andrés Manuel López Obrador, however, he did not hold a traditional joint press conference with them at the White House, an indication that disagreements remained among the three countries.

At the UN, the president also bragged that after the Afghanistan withdrawal, the United States was not at war for the first time in 20 years, despite the presence of thousands of American soldiers and special forces in Iraq, Syria, Somalia, and Yemen, as well those based abroad in friendly countries.

The president's second international trip was planned for late October to attend two climate summits. The first was the G20, whose members were those with the most advanced economies; the second was in Scotland for all members of the UN. The G20 summit was disappointing. Although verbiage for climate control remained strong, with net-zero carbon emissions the goal, the timetables countries adopted to meet this goal shifted with the needs and fossil fuel resources of the countries concerned. Russia had set 2060 as its date; Biden had previously proposed

2030 for the United States; the summit consensus year to achieve these goals was 2050. The conference also agreed to facilitate the distribution of COVID vaccines to 40 percent of the world's population by the end of 2021 and 70 percent the following year. They signed a joint communique, more goal oriented than policy specific, to support countries that phased out their investments in coal-based power plants. Keeping temperatures from increasing more than 1.5 percent Celsius was another objective that was part of the final communique.

The UN Climate Change Conference was held in Scotland, beginning the following week. Neither of the presidents of Russia nor China attended the meetings. Biden apologized for his predecessor's withdrawal from the Paris Climate Accord, made pledges of $300 million to help nations threatened by rising seas, and said the United States would contribute to reforestation and cut the amount of methane released into the environment. Biden also noted that $555 billion in the *Build Back Better* legislation was targeted to climate improvement.

More than 100 countries took a pledge to reduce methane emissions by half by the end of the decade. Countries also said that they would try to achieve a net-zero carbon policy, but their timeframes for doing so differed. Biden had promised a 50 percent reduction in greenhouse gases by 2030; Russia had proposed a reduction by 2060 and India by 2070, although India also requested a trillion dollars from advanced economies to enable it to do so.

The bottom line, however, was that everyone wanted to decrease threats to the warming environment, but they also had to consider their national needs: low energy prices, revenue from sale of fossil fuels, as well as national security concerns. Critics pointed out that Europe and the United States were the major polluters in previous centuries and that China, Russia, and India were today, as was the United States.

Nonetheless, the UN conferees agreed to meet the goals of the 2015 Paris Climate Accords in order to stop subsidizing fossil fuel to reduce rising temperatures. The United States and China announced a major agreement to take enhanced climate actions to slow the increase in temperature by 2 degrees Celsius (3.6 degrees Fahrenheit). At the same time, gas and oil prices were increasing, as many large oil-producing countries were limiting their supply for their future financial benefit.

After Biden returned from the summit, he ended up calling on Russia, Saudi Arabia, and the United Arab Emirates to produce more gas and oil to lower consumer prices, not exactly in the spirit of lowering carbon emissions. They did not do so. As a consequence, Biden released 50 million barrels of oil from the U.S. strategic reserve.

Nonetheless, oil prices continued to rise, electric utilities began to burn more coal, which was cheaper, and the pandemic increased car travel, with airlines, trains, and buses viewed as unsafe. Greenhouse gas emissions rose 6.8 percent in the year Biden attended the UN summit after he had pledged to reduce them, proposed climate legislation, and continued to institute executive agencies to do so.

In 2022, the president attended a NATO summit in which the Russian invasion of Ukraine was the principal topic. On the same trip, he went to Poland to meet American forces stationed there, Polish government officials, and refugees who had fled from Ukraine. In May, Biden traveled to Japan and Korea to meet with Korean and Japanese leaders as well as attended a QUAD summit with India, Japan, and Australia. At the end of June, he attended the G7 summit in Germany and the NATO summit in Spain.

In June, the White House also confirmed a trip to the Middle East planned for July in which the president will be at meetings with the leaders of Israel, the Palestinian Authority, and Saudi Arabia. The Saudi Arabian meeting with Crown Prince Mohammed bin Salman has provoked controversy in the United States because of Salman's alleged role in the killing of Jamel Khashoggi who became an American citizen and worked as a journalist for the *Washington Post.*

The New Biden Doctrine: Realism

Biden's initial foreign policy goals took time to establish. He saw the world divided between democratic and autocratic governments. He believed that democracy itself was under attack and sought to defend it, contending that democratic societies were capable of developing and defending their values and national interests. These values included personal freedom, press freedom, free and fair elections, and representative government. Biden saw threats to these values coming from nation states—China, Russia, Iran, and North Korea—international non-state-based terrorism, and worldwide health and climate issues.

Although democracy versus authoritarianism bookended his world view, it did not dictate his actions. Biden was a realist: progressive but flexible, principled but not overtly ideological. He also had to acknowledge the national interests of friends and foes alike. These interests required his administration to compromise and even make concessions, given the state of the world and American interests.

To achieve his goals, Biden had to confront international and domestic disunity: disunity among allies with similar values, mainly Western European countries; discord within the United States that threatened unified support for democratic values; and international problems so large and widespread that no country alone could resolve them, much less impose a world-wide solution.

The goals then were to strengthen democracies where possible, usually in countries that had developed, practiced, and valued the merits of a democratic society. To coordinate, consult, and design cooperative policies among these countries, essential to countering the growth and threats emanating from autocratic countries, democracies had to put themselves individually and collectively into a more competitive position to defend their security, territory, and policies.

Articulating this doctrine was easier for Biden and his defense and foreign policy advisors, almost all of whom had worked with him in the past and helped to shape his ideas, than achieving it. The world had changed dramatically in the last three decades with the rise of non-state-based terrorism; the growth of China's economic power, based in large part on its technological advances; the reemergence of Russia as a dominant player and power after the fall of the Soviet Union; the growing importance, wealth, and instability of the Middle East; and the continued poverty of much of the rest of the world. Fighting wars on terrorism, engaging in nation-building, and trying to impose democratic practices on religious and ethnic societies ruled by autocratic leaders with no history of democratic government all proved to be costly foreign policies with little gain and even less success for the so-called leader of the free world. Biden was sensitive to these international changes, which explains why he rejected the criticism that his foreign policy would be similar to that of the Obama administration but does not explain why he appointed as senior advisors people who were associated with the two previous Democratic administrations.

Relations With Allies and Adversaries

Friends

Many countries welcomed Biden's promise of multilateral diplomacy, the democratic values and practices he articulated, and the promise of

U.S. support against threats to their national interests and sovereignty. But they also wanted to protect and advance their own economic needs and agreements that they had made with Russia and China: an oil pipeline from Russia to Germany, the exports to a large Chinese market and imports of that country's advanced communication technologies, in addition to clamoring for the removal of U.S.-imposed tariffs on aluminum, iron, and steel that were initiated during the Trump administration and the COVID travel restrictions still in place that prevented travel to the United States. The travel restrictions for vaccinated visitors were lifted in early November 2021, as were the tariffs on aluminum and steel from the European Union.

Another problem was that all so-called democratic governments were not equally democratic. Some had autocratic, elected leaders; many of these leaders prevented dissent and punished dissenters; some subsidized industries that competed with U.S. corporations; others encouraged American businesses to move abroad by lowering the taxes they would pay in the United States. Immigration from the Middle East and northern Africa was also a contentious issue. These matters required the Biden administration to be realistic: to understand cultural variance, the internal political pressures that other governments faced, and competing national interests. It also required multilateral diplomacy, cooperative agreements, and strengthening military security against potential threats from adversaries, goals that were easier to achieve in theory than practice.

In September, a working group from the United Kingdom, Australia, and the United States began to design plans to share advanced technologies in an effort to improve their competitiveness with China. One product of the agreement was strengthening Australia's military capabilities by encouraging that country to purchase nuclear submarines built by U.S. defense contractors and terminating a multi-billion-dollar contract with France to build more traditional nonnuclear subs. The French were furious; they recalled their ambassadors to Australia and the United States in protest. President Biden initiated a call to French President Emmanuel Macron a few days later to try to rectify the situation. He promised more in-depth consultation with France in the future.

Foes

Being tough with Russia was a component of Biden's developing foreign policy doctrine. Russia was viewed negatively by three out of four

Americans at that time. Biden spoke with Putin twice in December, the first in a virtual visible call lasting two hours and the second in a nonvisible telephone call for 50 minutes. During the first conversation between the two presidents, Biden urged the use of diplomacy to end the Russian threat to Ukraine and also said that the United States would impose significant economic and security sanctions if Ukraine was invaded; Putin expressed his concern that NATO not expand eastward toward Russia, its allies, or other countries in Eastern Europe, countries that had been controlled by the Soviet Union. In the second call, Putin increased his demands on NATO, threatened a break in United States–Russian diplomatic relations if the United States imposed severe sanctions, and wanted American-supplied missiles removed from Ukraine. Biden conveyed the conversation to Ukraine's president the next day.

In 2022, diplomatic meetings were held on January 9 and 10 in Geneva, Switzerland, between Russian and American foreign policy and national security officials. After the weekend on January 12, U.S. representatives met with the Russian Council and entities from the Organization for Security and Co-operation in Europe, including Ukraine's president, Volodymyr Zelenskyy, on January 13.[3]

Photo 13.1 *Russian President Vladimir Putin talks with President Biden via a video call in December 2021*
Source: Mikhail Metzel, Sputnik, Kremlin Pool Photo via AP Photo

For Biden and the American people at that time, China was still viewed as the United States' principal rival. Public opinion perceived China as a greater threat to the U.S. economy, national security, and democratic values than Russia and viewed China even more unfavorably.[4] China's economic, technological, and territorial expansion were major issues that needed to be confronted, contained, and overcome competitively and cooperatively by the United States and its major Asian allies.

Biden did not alter Trump's China trade restrictions and tariffs on Chinese-made products; in fact, he added to his predecessor's list of Chinese companies in which Americans could not invest, pointing to an international digital agreement that excluded China, and continued cordial relations and trade with Taiwan. Deputy Secretary of State, Wendy Sherman, met with China's top foreign policy officials to discuss their concerns about each other's policies and actions. From the American perspective, the purpose of the sessions was to keep lines of communications open and to set parameters, "guardrails" not to be violated. The meeting was contentious; there was little accord.

Nonetheless, Biden did not want competition with China to turn into conflict. In a September 2021 address at the UN, he said: "We are not seeking a new Cold War, or a world divided into rigid blocks."[5] Trade Representative, Katherine Tai, said she would engage with Chinese leaders on trade relations but also reiterated U.S. objections to China's violation of international norms and agreements to gain economic advantage.

The Chinese were also miffed by the agreement that Australia would build nuclear submarines that had greater missile-launching capabilities, avoiding detection, and remaining submerged for longer periods. They saw the new agreement as an essential component in the strategic alliance by allied governments, led by the United States, that was designed to contain and control Chinese territorial expansion. The president held a virtual summit with Chinese President Xi Jinping on the evening of November 15; however, no joint communique was issued. Tensions with China were also increased with the disappearance of Chinese tennis star Peng Shuai, who had accused senior Chinese government officials of sexually assaulting her.

The rivalry with China, the continuing presence of U.S. forces in the Middle East, and the cooperative military strategy that followed from Biden's desire for joint alliance leadership and actions forced the administration to rethink its military strategy. In a war game that tested U.S. armed responses to international threats, tactical and strategic weaknesses were discovered that convinced the Secretary of Defense and military leaders to revise their war plans and overseas deployments. Additionally, the president's decision to withdraw U.S. combat forces first from Afghanistan and later from Iraq posed serious security issues and threatened the stability of American-backed governments in those countries, although one that did not initially generate much public concern in the United States.

Nonetheless, a majority of the American public favored the pullout. They had come to believe that the war was a mistake. Opinions were divided along partisan lines, with Democrats and Independents favoring Biden's decision and Republicans strongly opposing it.[6]

The withdrawal itself, however, was chaotic. Thirteen Americans and hundreds of Afghans died in a suicide bombing. A few Americans and thousands of Afghans were unable to leave. The American public criticized the implementation of the withdrawal, although they still favored doing it.[7] (See Box 13.1 for a description of the evacuation.)

Box 13.1 The Implementation of the Afghanistan Decision

Foreign policy experts at home and abroad were critical of the quick departure, the turmoil that they expected to ensue, and promises made by the Taliban to respect the rights, values, and practices of the Afghan people. Americans were aghast when they saw what was happening, especially the lines of desperate Afghans who had helped Americans trying to leave.

Biden's decision to withdraw was not precipitous. Before announcing it, he had consulted extensively with countries that also had troops in Afghanistan and had supported U.S. efforts. He had spoken with U.S. military commanders in Afghanistan, read reports from various intelligence agencies, and discussed the matter with the National Security Council. Those on the ground in Afghanistan urged caution. They feared that if U.S. military forces left the country, the Taliban would expand its territorial control, and the American-backed Afghan government would be unable to contain Taliban gains and might even collapse under pressure from its adversaries. Intelligence reports reinforced the military's judgment that a rapid withdrawal would increase internal conflict and jeopardize Afghans who aided the American effort, although the administration claimed that such reports did not predict such a quick or comprehensive collapse.[8] The president stuck with his decision and timeframe despite the cautions of the Secretaries of Defense and State that more time was needed to complete the operation satisfactorily.[9]

Such a rapid withdrawal required coordination with the leadership of the combatants. Face-saving meetings with Afghanistan's president and Iraq's prime minister were scheduled in July in the White House to inform them of the decision, reiterate America's continued support for their governments' goals and anti-terrorism policies, and obtain their positive response to the actions the United States was about to take. Secret negotiations with the Taliban were conducted to minimize violence, particularly retaliation against Americans and Afghans who wanted to leave the country. U.S. representatives provided the Taliban with names of American citizens, green card holders, and Afghan allies so that they would be allowed to enter the airport gates.

Giving the Taliban a list of people who had aided the American effort outraged members of Congress and military officials who did not trust the Taliban and feared the information would put individuals on the list, especially friendly Afghans, in danger. Nonetheless, security talks with the Taliban continued during the withdrawal.

The fears of Americans who opposed a hasty military withdrawal were quickly and painfully realized as the press reported Taliban advances, the collapse of Afghanistan's security forces, and finally, the fall of the government itself.

Panic ensued. Thousands of Afghans rushed to the only airfield, Kabul International Airport, left open by the Americans. Flights had to be arranged; temporary facilities to feed, house, and care for the refugees set up; papers and documents that testified to their status examined and verified; and permission to enter the United States given. Many of these requirements could not be done quickly. The Trump administration had purposely slowed the State Department's refugee approval process, reducing its staff to interview, vet, and resettle refugees, a process that the Biden administration had difficulty reversing within its first six months in office. Front-line State Department officials were overwhelmed and disorganized, trying to help Americans and Afghans who wanted to leave the country.

They were also unclear about their own authority, and what they could and could not do to help people leave the country.[10]

The need to remove all Americans who wished to leave Afghanistan required the U.S. embassy in Kabul to notify its diplomats, contractors, and Afghan workers. They were urged to go to the airport immediately. Many were stopped and accosted by Taliban security personnel, thereby requiring teams of special forces to try to rescue them. To establish order at the airport, an additional 6,000 American soldiers and Marines from nearby Middle East bases were rushed to the scene. The chaos, captured by international news media, revealed heartbreaking stories and pictures of panicked Afghans packed wall-to-wall in intense summer heat, standing inside and outside the American-controlled air field.

As the evacuation was unfolding, U.S. and allied intelligence warned of attacks against those who wanted and needed to leave. Infighting among various Afghan militia groups was reported, and days later, a suicide bomber from a rival group to the Taliban, ISIS-K, killed and wounded hundreds of people, Americans, Afghans, and foreign nationals, waiting outside one of the airport's gates. In a reprisal attack, a drone armed with a missile destroyed a car allegedly carrying terrorists; however, the intelligence about the car's occupants was incorrect. Ten civilians, including seven children, lost their lives. The Defense Department ordered an investigation and ultimately paid compensation to the victims' families.

Biden's National Security Council met in emergency sessions throughout the withdrawal period. The administration was clearly put on the defensive; friendly foreign governments questioned its understanding of the complexity of the situation and its cooperative leadership policy in light of what seemed like an "America First" decision. The press reported stories and pictures of frightened Afghans who wanted to leave. Nonetheless, the administration claimed the decision was correct, that 125,000 people had been evacuated by the United States and its allies, and 70,000 Afghans who worked for the United States and their families were to be admitted to the United States after they received their papers and background checks. They were transferred to American military bases in Europe and the Middle East.

The administration's judgment and the president's attributes of empathy, fairness, and concern for human rights were damaged. Biden's immunity from personal criticism ended. Republicans called for his removal and even questioned his mental agility. Democratic reaction ranged from outrage to anguish, with five congressional investigations of the evacuation underway by mid-September 2021. European leaders criticized the decision.

Along with the surge of immigrants and the spread of the Delta and Omicron COVID variants, court decisions that overturned some his executive actions, and the internal divisions within the Democratic Party over the scope of its policy agenda, the summer of 2021 began a decline in public support for the Biden presidency.[11]

Political and Economic Consequences

The debacle in Afghanistan highlighted the dangers of recalibrating Middle East policy. It also had implications for implementing new foreign policy priorities, mobilizing coalitional support for political and economic gain, and resisting Russian and Chinese incursions that threated U.S. interests. Biden found that actions speak louder than words, that results and conditions matter more than promises and hopeful policy reforms.

By the end of the year, it was unclear how a recalibration of policy toward Saudi Arabia, growing Iranian influence, and the removal of American forces would affect security in the Middle East. The buildup of Russian military forces at the Ukrainian border became another serious threat that the president had to address. The Biden Doctrine was flexible, but it did not promote his democratic principles and environmental concerns as much as he desired.

Russia invaded Ukraine on February 24 after the Olympic Games in China ended.

President Biden said that the United States would not send combat forces to Ukraine but would supply defensive weapons. He rushed American military forces to the Ukrainian border and urged other NATO countries to do so as well. He denounced the Russian aggression and called the Russian president "a war criminal." Biden later said that Putin could not remain in power, a remark that the White House clarified by saying that "the president meant that the Russian leader could not exercise power over the region."[12]

As the war progressed, Biden did not soften his criticism of President Putin. He urged Congress to appropriate additional funds to help Ukraine. By May 20, 2022, $54 billion for military and humanitarian assistance had been appropriated.[13] The next month the president asked Congress for $1 billion more for Ukraine.

Notes

1. According to a Pew Research Center survey of February 24, 2021, "60% of U.S. adults expressed confidence in Biden on foreign policy—fewer than said the same of Barack Obama as his presidency began (74%) but more than for Donald Trump in his first year (46%)." "Majority of Americans Confident in Biden's Handling of Foreign Policy as Term Begins," *Pew Research Center*, February 24, 2021.
2. Julie Ray, "US Approval Ratings Rally from Record Low," *Gallup Poll*, October 19, 2021.
3. Robyn Dixon and Paul Sonne, "Putin: Ties with U.S. at Stake Over Ukraine," *Washington Post*, December 31, 2021.
4. "Trends A–Z: Country Ratings," *Gallup Poll*.
5. Joe Biden, "Remarks by President Biden at the United Nations General Assembly," *White House*, September 21, 2021.
6. Megan Brena, "Americans Split on Whether Afghanistan War Was a Mistake," *Gallup Poll*, July 26, 2021; Ted Van Green and Carroll Doherty, "Majority of U.S. Public Favors Afghanistan Withdrawal; Biden Criticized for His Handling of Situation," *Pew Research Center*, August 31, 2021.
7. Van Green and Doherty, "Majority of U.S. Public Favors Afghanistan Withdrawal; Biden Criticized for His Handling of Situation."
8. Mark Mazzetti, Julian E. Barnes, and Adam Goldman, "Intelligence Warned of Afghan Military Collapse, Despite Biden's Assurances," *New York Times*, August 20, 2021.
9. Bob Woodward and Robert Costa, *Peril* (New York, NY: Simon and Schuster, 2021).
10. Katasha Korecki and Nahal Toosi, "This Experience Broke a Lot of People: Inside State Amid the Afghanistan Withdrawal," *Politico*, November 17, 2021. See also "Five Desperate Days Escaping Kabul," *New York Times*, December 24, 2021.
11. See also "Five Desperate Days Escaping Kabul," *New York Times*, December 24, 2021.
12. Ashley Parker and Tyler Page, "Biden: Putin Cannot Remain in Power," *Washington Post*, March 27, 2022.
13. Bianca Pallaro and Allcia Partapiano, "Four Ways to Understand the $54 Billion in U.S. Spending on Ukraine," *New York Times,* May 20, 2022.

CHAPTER 14

AN EVALUATION OF THE BIDEN PRESIDENCY

In his campaign, Biden promised to protect democratic values, promote domestic unity within the country and cooperative leadership abroad, cope with the pandemic, revitalize the economy, improve racial relations, reform immigration policies and procedures, reduce the harmful effects of climate change, and expand health care. He also pledged to restore normalcy in the presidency, foster bipartisanship in his relations with Congress, and not intrude on the independence of the Justice Department. How well did Biden achieve these intended goals?

Assessing the Biden Presidency: Major Policy Change but Increased Political Polarization

There are various ways to evaluate a presidency: measuring the president's promises and performance in office; the president's job approval ratings; changes in the economic, social, and political environment; and the public's trust and confidence in the government and satisfaction with the direction in which the country is heading.

Promises and Performance

Biden promised to tame the pandemic, restore economic growth, improve the climate, reform immigration, decrease inequality, increase educational and professional opportunities for minorities and first-generation Americans, maintain law and order including investigating misconduct by police, and protect the nation's democratic values, economic interests, and national security. He achieved some but certainly not all of these goals in his first 18 months in office.

DOI: 10.4324/9781003176978-19

Congress enacted two of his major legislative priorities, the *American Rescue Plan Act of 2021* and the bipartisan infrastructure bill. The Biden administration promoted vaccinations, social distancing, and mask wearing to reduce the number of infections from the COVID-19 virus. The Food and Drug Administration approved more vaccines for more age groups, including booster shots, and the White House and government health agencies communicated more information about the disease and the best ways to try to avoid it.

Biden urged people to get vaccinated, and his White House oversaw the rapid distribution of vaccines that had successfully gone through the standard FDA review process. Government officials encountered more difficulty in designing accurate testing methods. They encouraged more people to agree to be vaccinated. A strong anti-vaccination movement coalesced among people who did not believe in vaccinations, questioning the scientific evidence on which they were based and the protocols that had to be followed for approval, fearing long-term health issues that could result from a quickly developed vaccine. There was political opposition as well, fostered by strong partisan and ideological views based on freedom of choice, suspicion of government, and misinformation. The opposition extended to mask wearing and social distancing. About 23 percent of Americans remain unvaccinated. (See weekly CDC Covid-19 tracker.) As new variants of the virus reached the United States, the people not vaccinated have disproportionately suffered.

The president's response to the renewed threat of infection by the Delta, Omicron, and other variants of the COVID virus has been require vaccinations, testing, and masks for government employees and contractors, people on federal property, private sector businesses that employed more than 100 people, and riders on public interstate transit. The president's action, though supported by a majority of the population, heightened political tensions, spurred legal challenges, and evoked state policies by some conservative Republican governors who opposed Biden's policies and actions. The pandemic continued; getting back to normal remained a hope, not an accomplishment. Biden had claimed success too soon.

President Biden partially redeemed some of his climate goals in his proposals that were incorporated in the bipartisan infrastructure bill that he helped negotiate and get enacted into law. Other legislative climate initiatives placed in the *Build Back Better* legislation were not achieved when the Senate failed to pass the bill. Through executive actions and international commitments, Biden also sought to address climate change. He ordered departments and agencies to regulate harmful emissions going into the atmosphere, toxic discharges into waters, and discriminatory policies that adversely impacted minority communities. But there was more to do, and environmentalists exerted more pressure on him to address these issues. Other issues, however, received higher priority, such as rising energy prices. Moreover, the president's climate goals required support from other countries and private sector companies whose actions he could not command or control.

The Biden administration had less success in enhancing democratic values and practices, reducing income inequality, and preventing discriminatory behaviors against minorities. His words condemned but were unable to stop these incidents from occurring.

Presidential Job Approval

For the first six months, the president's job approval ratings were more favorable than unfavorable. Over time, however, the president's popularity was tied to external conditions, conditions that he had not been able to improve. As the pandemic persisted, economic growth slowed, inflation spiked, criticism of the president increased, and Democratic unity splintered. Biden's job approval ratings fell into the negative range. Disapproval topped approval by more than 10 percent.

The withdrawal from Afghanistan contributed to the president's lower ratings. Biden, who ordered the withdrawal, suffered the consequences. His timing, judgment, and competence were questioned. The president's mental agility and foresight became subjects of debate. When combined with his difficulties in controlling the pandemic, restoring the economy without inflating it, and unifying his party's base, the public perceived Biden as floundering, unable to meet multiple tasks, and having inadequate leadership skills. Republicans were heartened as they looked toward the 2022 midterm elections; Democrats were dismayed; Biden had become the target of discontent.

Although more than 50 percent of registered voters approved of the job he was doing during his first six months in office, that percentage dropped during the next year into the low 40s. (See Tables 12.1 and 12.2.) Public opinion of many of his policy positions and his personal attributes also declined.

Changes in the Economic, Social, and Political Environment

Optimism turned to pessimism about conditions in the country. Although the economy improved but not to its pre-pandemic levels, public confidence in it did not. The stimulus payments and low interest rates kept the stock market strong until inflation spiked and reduced unemployment but also increased demand while pandemic-related manufacturing and distribution problems reduced supply and raised the cost of living. Perceptions of the economy worsened along with outlooks about its future. (See Table 14.1.)

Social discord remained. Togetherness was not achieved. Divisions among groups framed by longtime cultural biases and discriminatory practices were difficult to overcome. Minorities suffered the most.

Biden's first year inflamed but did not change the political climate. The country stayed deeply polarized along partisan and ideological lines, while the partisan parity between the major parties continued and the gap between the number of people who identified as conservative and liberal narrowed. Democrats overwhelmingly supported Biden's stance on the issues, and Independents also tilted toward him, but Republicans

TABLE 14.1 Confidence in the Economy (in percent)

Time Span	Current Conditions			Economic Outlook		
	Excellent/ Good	Fair	Poor	Getting Better	Getting Worse	Same
January 4–15, 2021	28	39	33	29	66	3
February 3–18	20	49	31	39	54	4
March 1–15	23	46	31	44	50	6
April 1–21	28	46	26	47	46	4
May 3–18	27	42	30	43	53	5
June 1–18	30	43	26	47	50	3
July 6–21	30	45	27	41	54	4
August 2–17	28	42	29	37	60	3
September 1–17	25	39	35	32	65	3
October 1–19	25	42	33	27	68	4
November 1–16	22	42	36	26	70	4
December 1–16	18	40	42	26	67	1
January 1–16, 2022	23	40	37	29	67	4
February 1–17	21	37	42	26	70	3
March 1–18	22	35	44	20	75	3
April 1–19	20	38	42	20	76	3
May 2–22	14	39	46	20	77	2
June 1–20	12	34	54	13	85	2

Source: "Topics A–Z: The Economy," *Gallup Poll*, 2021–2022

strongly opposed his policies and their implementation. Perceptions of his personal attributes were similarly affected by the public's partisan and ideological orientations. As the first year progressed, these evaluations among partisans shifted, but not to the president's advantage.

Trust and Confidence in the Government and Its Leadership

Trust in government is an important factor in assessing a presidency. During Biden's first year in office, it declined even further than the low levels it had reached during Trump's first year. Only 8 percent of Americans had a great deal of trust in government, 31 percent a fair amount, and a whopping 70 percent little or none at all, with Democrats feeling the government was more trustworthy than Republicans and Independents. The decline was even steeper at the end of 18 months with only 20 percent trusting the government in Washington always or most of the time; in 1960, the level of trust was 79 percent and it has declined steadily except right after the 9/11 terrorist attacks.[1]

Trust correlates with partisanship. Partisans of the party controlling the White House have higher levels of trust than Independents and those of identifying or leaning toward other parties. At the end of Biden's first 18 months, 29 percent of Democrats but only 9 percent of Republican trusted the government always or most of the time.[2]

Confidence in governing institutions has also declined with the steepest decrease the Spreme Court after its Roe v. Wade decision. Table 14.2 indicates confidence levels during Biden's first six months.

Satisfaction with the direction the country was heading also decreased. At the beginning of Biden's first year, 27 percent were satisfied with the way

Table 14.2 Confidence in Government Institutions (in percent)

Presidency			Congress			Supreme Court		
Great Deal	Some	Very Little	Great Deal	Some	Very Little	Great Deal	Some	Very Little
Quite a Lot		None	Quite a Lot		None	Quite a Lot		None
38	29	33	12	37	54	51	36	42

(Continued)

TABLE 14.2 (Continued)

(September 2021)

	Executive Branch	Judicial System	Legislature
Great Deal	17	10	5
Fair Amount	27	44	32
Not Very Much	56	46	62

Source: "Topics A–Z: Confidence in Institution," *Gallup Poll,* 2021

TABLE 14.3 Satisfaction with the United States (in percent)

Time Frame	Satisfied	Dissatisfied	No Opinion
January 4–15	11	88	1
February 3–18	27	71	1
March 1–15	32	67	1
April 1–21	34	65	1
May 3–18	36	62	2
June 1–18	35	63	7
July 6–21	30	69	1
August 2–17	23	77	1
September 1–17	24	75	1
October 1–19	23	75	1
November 1–16	24	73	1
December 1–16	21	79	1
January 3–16 (2022)	17	82	1
February 1–17	21	78	1
March 1–18	24	75	1
April 1–19	22	77	1
May 2–22	16	83	1
June 1–20	13	87	–

Source: Gallup Poll, 2021–2022

things were going in the United States and 77 percent were dissatisfied. By mid-June 2022, the percentages had dropped to 13 who were satisfied with 87 still dissatisfied. Trump's first year figures were 30 percent satisfied and 68 percent dissatisfied at the beginning of his presidency and 29 percent satisfied and 68 percent dissatisfied at the end of it. (See Table 14.3.)

The Biden Scoreboard

What the Biden administration tried to accomplish and did or did not achieve, how it carried out its responsibilities, and the unresolved issues can also be used to evaluate his presidency. In the eyes of the public, that evaluation was mixed and shifted over the course of the year.

Table 14.4 provides a scoreboard of Biden's major successes and failures for his first 18 months in office.

Biden had both successes and failures since he took office. He achieved two of his principal legislative goals and exercised executive powers to achieve other major policy objectives. His appointees met with public approval but did so along partisan lines. The president's bipartisan approach also met with mixed success.

In the foreign policy arena, Biden stood up to adversarial leaders and enhanced America's reputation abroad. He directed the American response

TABLE 14.4 The Biden Scoreboard

Successes	Failures
Executive Actions	
Allowed more immigrants to enter the United States legally	Unable to stop the flood of immigrants entering the country illegally
Raised the minimum wage for federal contractors to $15 an hour	Unable to persuade Congress to enact new national minimum wage legislation from $7.25 per hour
Decreased unemployment	Increased inflation
Increased vaccination rates substantially and made free home testing available	Sometimes provided confusing information on COVID-19 testing and treatments
Ended U.S. military involvement in Afghanistan	Chaotic withdrawal from Afghanistan
Cancelled $5.8 billion in students loans for 560 thousand former Corinthian College students	Unable to agree on student loan forgiveness for 43 million other American students
Provided aid to Ukraine	Unable to stop Russian military aggression in Ukraine
Major Legislation	
The American Rescue Plan Act of 2021	*U.S. Citizenship Act of 2021*
Infrastructure and Investment Act	*John R. Lewis Voting Rights Advancement Act of 2021*
Emmitt Till Anti-Lynching Act	*Freedom to Vote Act*
Postal Reform Act of 2022	*Build Back Better Act*
Leadership Skills	
Steady and deliberative decision-making	Alleged insularity of president and senior advisors and "groupthink" mentality on some issues
Bipartisan and partisan compromises	Concessions on promised Democratic agenda
Empathetic, caring, and friendly	Strength, assertiveness, and energizing
Judgment based on scientific evidence	Incorrect factual claims in public remarks

to Russia's invasion of Ukraine and persuaded Congress to appropriate large sums of money.

There were no terrorist attacks within the United States, but hacking by foreign countries and individuals and organizations within them continued to be a security problem. Biden responded appropriately to natural disasters and enhanced the status of the presidency in the eyes of the American people and most of the rest of the world. He ended America's military involvement in Afghanistan, but the Taliban took control of that country's government and the withdrawal was chaotic and lives were lost.

Domestically, the Biden administration improved testing and distribution of COVID vaccines but it also fueled political discord with the president's mask mandates. Some of the administration's public communications on coping with the pandemic were inconsistent and confusing. Jobs increased and unemployment reached a new low, but inflation spiked. Biden began with positive job approval ratings in his first six months, but they then declined during the summer and continued to drop throughout his first 18 months in office.

Photo 14.1 *President Biden travels to Poland in March 2022 to speak about the Russia–Ukraine war*
Source: AP Photo/Evan Vucci

Why the steep decline? Conditions worsen; the pandemic continued, even the president caught the COVID virus; inflation reached new heights, 9.5 percent in June 2022, the largest increase in 41 years; and the economy weakened, a forthcoming recession loomed in the foreseeable future. The Russian invasion of Ukraine, the sanctions the United States imposed, supply chain shortages, all with no end in sight, contributed to the public's malaise. The partisan and cultural wars continued with heated rhetoric as the midterm elections approached. Promises that the president made in his campaign, inauguration, and the early days of his administration remained partially or completely unfilled. Nor did most Americans see the physical improvements that the bipartisan infrastructure bill was designed to achieve.

Relief that Biden won the 2020 election turned to dismay over the president's leadership skills. When multiple problems near crisis proportions people look to the president for help, hope, and change. Being a nice guy – friendly, cooperative, compassionate, honest, ethical, and empathic – is not enough. People want strong leadership that produces concrete results. Biden's personal traits deemed positively by the electorate in 2020 turned negative after 6 months in office. His age, gaffes, factual mistakes, and slow responses to continuing health, economic, social, and environmental concerns contributed to the perception that an octogenarian president was not up to the job and should not run for reelection. From the public's perspective, the Emperor still had clothes, but his presidential garb was becoming tarnished and did not fit nearly as well as it did during his first six months in office.

What grade would you give him?

Perceptions change slowly as do external conditions, except in times of crisis. The summer of 2021 marked the beginning of public discontent with the Biden administration. One year later, several hopeful signs for the administration began to appear. Gas prices dropped; job growth continued to be strong, and unemployment remained low; the stock market responded positively to the Federal Reserve's increase in interest rates. Although the BA. 2 variant of the COVID virus spread rapidly across the country, hospitalizations and deaths declined. Ayman al-Zawahri, an al-Qaida terrorist leader responsible for planning the 911 and other the bombings, was killed by a U.S. drone attack.

Congress enacted a substantial portion of the Build Back Better legislation in a law, titled the Inflation Reduction Act. The legislation contained $369 billion for climate and energy improvement, tax credits for the purchase of electric vehicles, price reductions for some prescription drugs negotiated by Medicare with drug manufacturers, limits on yearly out-of-pocket prescription costs for Medicare recipients, and extended subsidies for low and middle income Americans insured by the Affordable Care Act. A minimum corporate tax was established to generate the revenue to pay for the bill with left-over funds intended to reduce the national debt. Congress also passed laws to boost U.S. competition with China, subsidize the manufacturing of computer chips, and help veterans who suffered burn-related injuries during their active duty service. Democrats hoped the legislation would boost their chances in the midterm elections; Republicans saw increased government spending contributing to the inflation. It was a victory for Biden, but whether it would enhance his political standing in the eyes of the public remained unclear.

Notes

1. "Trust in Government Hits Historic Lows," *Pew Research Center*, June 6, 2022.
2. Ibid.

Appendix: Most important problems (in percent)

	Winter 2021		Spring 2021			Summer 2021			Fall 2021			Winter 2022			Spring 2022		
	February	March	April	May	June	July	August	September	October	November	December	January	February	March	April	May	June
Economic Problems	19	16	21	19	21	23	20	18	16	24	25	22	30	35	39	37	40
Government/ Poor Leadership	29	19	20	14	16	22	18	16	19	21	21	21	20	22	20	19	18
COVID-19	20	26	25	20	15	8	12	26	21	15	13	13	13	3	4	2	1
Immigration	1	3	8	14	12	9	8	11	7	11	9	7	4	5	7	8	5
Race Relations	10	10	8	12	11	11	9	4	5	5	5	6	4	5	4	5	5
Situation with Russia												*	2	9	5	3	1

Source: "Topics A–Z: Most Important Problem," *Gallup Poll*, 2021–2022*

Index

Note: Page numbers in *italics* indicate a figure and page numbers in **bold** indicate a table.